Responsive Labor

RESPONSIVE LABOR

A Theology of Work

David H. Jensen

Westminster John Knox Press
LOUISVILLE • LONDON

Book design by Sharon Adams
Cover design by Mark Abrams

First edition
Published by Westminster John Knox Press
Louisville, Kentucky

This book is printed on acid-free paper that meets the American National Standards Institute Z39.48 standard. ♾

PRINTED IN THE UNITED STATES OF AMERICA

06 07 08 09 10 11 12 13 14 15—10 9 8 7 6 5 4 3 2 1

Library of Congress Cataloging-in-Publication Data is on file at the Library of Congress, Washington, D.C.

ISBN-13: 978-0-664-23021-0
ISBN-10: 0-664-23021-0

For Finn

Contents

Preface

Daily work matters for Christian faith. Our ordinary labors—cleaning, cooking, caring for children, teaching, writing, investing, sculpting, trading, and building—are responses to the life God gives to the world. Christian faith is distinctive in its claim that the ordinary materials and practices of life are charged with the holy. Basic foods of bread and wine become the body and blood of Christ in a holy meal; ordinary human flesh becomes Emmanuel in a first-century carpenter, a man who worked with his hands; water, basic and indispensable to life, becomes the promise of new birth in ecclesial assembly; ordinary people gathered around Word and Sacrament become the church, the Body of Christ in the world. Bodies, baths, meals, and labor are central to Christian faith. In the incarnation of Jesus Christ and through the animating and sustaining power of the Holy Spirit, God takes these ordinary things as God's own and gives them to us, endowed with new life. Human work is not incidental to faith, but bound up with its chief movements. The basic topics of Christian theology, after all, can be described in terms of God's work for the world: creation, covenant, incarnation, justification, sanctification, and consummation. Christian theology describes these patterns of God's work for the life of the world, drawing us into communion with God, summoning our work as a response to that relationship. One claim of this book is that meaningful human work *responds* to the divine work that pulses at the heart of the universe. Though God's work is not dependent on ours, when our labors respond to the divine work, we also contribute to the life of the world.

Though work matters for Christian faith, it is easy for us to overestimate its value. Throughout history, humanity—and the church—have fallen captive to the idea that in work we create ourselves. The modern slogan, "You are what you do," merely echoes sentiments that have abided throughout the ages. We often place inordinate weight on our work: finding the "right" job, desiring to make our mark, wanting to do best for our children. Believing these slogans, our tendency at times is to believe that we can never work too much, that there is always something more to do, some way to improve our labors in God's sight and in others'. The good news of Christian faith, however, is that we do not create or justify ourselves through work; rather, by grace God claims us, names us, and makes us God's own. Reformation teaching is particularly adamant on this point: because God is already at work for us, we can rest in God's grace. If Christian faith claims that work matters, it also prohibits us from attributing too much significance to our earthly labors. Though we are made to work, work is not our chief end.

If good work responds to God's work for us, then our habits of daily work often fall short of this aim. We live in a world where work often becomes drudgery, where many who desire paid employment are denied access to meaningful work, where some control and own the labors of others, where white-collar workers become addicted to work while others languish in unemployment lines, where job satisfaction deteriorates, where backbreaking and exhausting work eclipses Sabbath. Human beings often experience work as alienation; indeed, as the biblical creation stories note, one of the first consequences of sin is that God-given work degenerates into toil (Gen. 3:17–19). Christian faith, therefore, cannot glimpse work through rose-tinted glasses, but recognizes the travail we often make of our labors. The work of human creatures is decidedly fallen work. But even this recognition does not obscure the hope that lies at the center of Christian faith: in Jesus Christ all of creation—even our work—is redeemed. The new reign inaugurated in Christ's work beckons the consummation of the world, where labors of war are transformed into the harmony of peace, where no one will hurt or destroy on God's holy mountain (Isa. 11:9).

This book aims to recover a Christian theological vision of ordinary work, a vision that grounds human labor in God's initiating activity. Human work has meaning as it responds to and lives from the triune God. As a whole, the present study is difficult to pigeonhole among the several genres of theological writing. At its most basic level, this is a work in constructive or doctrinal theology: I sketch a portrait of human work that draws on some of the classic doctrines, such as Trinity, sin and redemption, creation and consummation. But its topic—human labor—is rather foreign to most systematic theologies. Not often have the codifiers of Christian doctrine explored the topic of work as an explicitly theological theme. This oversight is significant, because it suggests that the bulk of the Christian life—time spent working—is at best tangential to the more basic claims of the faith. One impetus for this study is to counteract this tendency that marginalizes work in the life of Christian faith. As I see it, because Jesus of Nazareth assumes our flesh, because we meet God in him, we can confidently affirm that God takes all of our lives—in their ordinariness, in their work—as God's own. Doctrinal theology should not flee from work as if the only time that has meaning is away from work; rather, it should infuse our daily labors with a sense of God's presence within them.[1]

My study differs from much doctrinal theology by beginning not with a general account of God's activity or revelation, but by describing the pain of work in a North American context. The book, in other words, diagnoses a problem in our vision of work by suggesting how work falls short. In this sense, the book also fits the genre of practical theology as it summons theological resources to address dilemmas and realities of daily life. Finally, the book also makes a stab at liturgical theology, as it considers Christian worship one of the chief designators of meaningful work. The rhythms of liturgy, accordingly, offer gestures for the renewal of our daily labor. Throughout the whole study, however, ethical criteria leap to the fore. Sound doctrinal theology is not merely descriptive, but attempts to make normative claims as God's people live out faith in a broken world. As the study offers a theological portrait for human work, it also presents concrete suggestions for how our alienated labors might more closely correspond to the summons of God's reign.

The book comprises five chapters. In the first I survey some of the problems and promises of work in a U.S. context. A theology of work must pay attention to the context of American workers; otherwise, it spouts platitudes devoid of the nitty-gritty realities that face working people. The chapter does not provide an exhaustive study of America at work, but it does explore selected themes of unemployment/underemployment, the working poor, job satisfaction, overwork, and the gradual eclipse of leisure. Many of these realities of work in the United States stand in contrast to the free promises of the Christian gospel.

Chapter 2 turns to the history of Christian thought as a resource for valuing daily work. Even if work has rarely emerged in that history as an explicit theological topic, voices across the ages have grappled with work's ambiguity. In our varied traditions, human labor has been dismissed as a curse, heralded as a blessing, hearkened as a calling, and celebrated as cocreative with divine work. The chapter draws on a wide range of material, including biblical narratives, early monasticism, Reformation critiques, and papal encyclicals, as well as voices at the dawn of the new millennium. Views of work most appropriate for our age are those capable of acknowledging both the peril and promise of human labor.

In chapter 3 I turn more directly to doctrinal theology. The meaning and purpose of human work, I argue, is grounded in the work of the triune God.

The Trinity is a fundamentally practical doctrine, expressing God's work in the economy of redemption and our lives as taken, claimed, and blessed by God. Before we ever begin our earthly labors, God is already at work for us, informing and shaping our work. The consequences of this Trinitarian exploration of labor are wide-ranging and include the importance of shared labor, cooperative work, the valuing of distinctive work, the honoring of different workers, and the significance of play in the midst of work. In a context where work is hoarded, many are out of work, and others are overworked, these theological reflections offer practical suggestions for the revitalization and reordering of human work.

Chapter 4 takes up themes in liturgical theology. Worship reorients us to God's work as it claims us as participants in the life of the world. In worship, God gives Godself; we respond, in part by giving some of ourselves, represented in bread and wine that are the products of human labor. By bringing these gifts to God, God takes them, blesses them, and keeps on giving. In this eucharistic economy, we catch a glimpse of inexhaustible giving and the blessing of our imperfect labors. Jesus' gestures at the Lord's Table, accordingly, offer hope for the transformation of our work.

The final chapter turns to systemic issues in the U.S. economy. A theology of work would be incomplete were there not some examination of the economic engine that drives American workers. The chapter does not provide a blueprint for putting the aforementioned theological principles into practice; rather, it offers a theological critique of some aspects of American economic life and presents some general themes for renewing a sense of good work in that economy. The chapter critiques the extremes of global capitalism and socialism that ultimately denigrate workers and puts forth some alternative paradigms—subsidiarity and covenantal ethics—from Catholic and Reformed traditions. Though the problems and issues outlined in the first chapter are addressed throughout the book, this final chapter offers the most explicit response to the pain of work in North America.

My own work on this project has occurred intermittently. It has been patched together between the loving and mundane acts of diaper changing, teaching, bedtime story reading, cooking, carpool driving, and late-night conversation with the woman I love. Every step of the mind-wracking and creative activity of writing has been informed by these other precious labors. Good work, I am convinced, cannot occur in isolation, but is open to being changed by the faces of the others with whom we share work.

For the completion of this project, I have many to thank. Austin Seminary provided the sabbatical that made this work's completion a reality. Allan Cole and Stan Hall were generous with reading suggestions. Scott Black Johnston, Michael Jinkins, and Ellis Nelson helped me navigate the terrain of grant writing. The Louisville Institute's Christian Faith and Life Grant allowed me sufficient resources for the research and writing of this project, without which the book would not have appeared in print. The Southwest Regional Commission on Religious Studies Junior Scholar Award also enhanced this project in many ways. Conversations at the annual gathering of the Workgroup in Constructive Theology have stimulated my thinking far beyond our weekend meetings and embodied collaborative work. In retreat and class settings at St. Mark Lutheran Church, Salem, Oregon; University Presbyterian Church, Westlake Hills Presbyterian Church, and Trinity United Methodist Church, Austin; parishioners aided me in thinking through themes of work and vocation. Dean Pogue and Steve Vittorini provided lively exchanges in independent study projects. Reno Lauro helped this project in its infancy with his extensive bibliographic searches. Dhawn Martin has been a research assistant extraordinaire, pushing me in directions I would not have pursued otherwise. Consultations with scholars, pastors, businesspeople, and civic leaders in the United States and England were invaluable as I explored themes in lay vocation, sociology, public policy, philosophy, and economics, so thanks go to Max Sherman, Gretchen Webber, Paul Woodruff, Mike Murray, Ray Marshall, Gus García, Michael Ledzion, Martin Clark, Jim Griffiths, Andrew Glover, Richard Higginson, and Judy and Hal Boyd. Don McKim, an encouraging and thoughtful editor, showed a keen interest in the project at an early stage and urged me to write an accessible theological text.

Molly Hadley Jensen remains the book's greatest inspiration. In our shared labors of making a home, caring for children, and shaping a life together, we have also juggled the calling to meaningful work that extends beyond immediate family. These labors have never been seamless or easy, but when shared in a partnership they became occasions of joy. Hannah Grace teaches me to laugh while I work and calls me home. Finn, who arrived in the world as my labors on this project were wrapping up, reminds me that the first word in rest and at work is "thanks." To him, whose work is now play, the project is dedicated.

I hope that the reflections contained in this volume offer one approach for how Christians might reclaim notions of meaningful work in daily life, in ways faithful to theological traditions and attuned to dilemmas of the frenzied pace of life in the new millennium. Constructing this book, no doubt, has affected my own attitudes toward work: I am now more convinced than ever that there is no such thing as work that belongs to one person alone. Though the words on these pages are ones that I have composed, the labors behind the words have been shared with many.

1

Life's Labors

The Problem and Promise of Work in America

Human persons work the world over. Wherever there are people, one can find people working. Work is a reality so basic to life—like eating, sexuality, communication, and reproduction—that it appears as nonnegotiable to the human condition. However we may seek to avoid it, work will find us and we will find work. In many cases work is a matter of survival: to acquire daily bread, one tends the soil or works in some other trade to enjoy the fruits of a soil-tiller's labor. We work, in most cases, in order to live. But work cannot be considered only a means to survival since it can also be a form of self-expression: human labor gives birth to igloos and cathedrals; Navajo rugs and Ghanian kente cloth; novels and vaccinations; music and worship. In work, people create culture, identity, and even respond to the God who creates and renews all things. When work responds to the Creator, when it becomes something more than a means to securing the basic necessities of life, persons also can live, at least in part, to work.[1] Human labors, of course, are enormously varied and difficult to define. Depending on the circumstances of the worker, the same tasks can be expressions of joy or sorrow; what represents creative work for one may translate into drudgery for another; we often work because we are compelled to work, but at other times we may work out of a genuine sense of freedom. Given the sheer amount of time that persons spend working, it is surprising that Christian theologians have not addressed work more frequently as a theological topic.

If Christian theology, at one level, is the attempt to make sense of human life in light of God's gift—and work—for the world in Jesus Christ, then it needs to pay attention to the practice that occupies the bulk of most persons' waking hours: daily work. Too often, however, doctrinal theology has made the opposite assumption: what "really matters" for the life of faith is the time

1

spent away from work: in church, in prayer, in contemplation. The tragic consequence of this oversight is the tendency among Christians, regardless of denominational tradition, to separate faith from work. When the trades we ply from Monday through Friday have little bearing on faith confessed Sunday morning, when that confession hovers on the surface of weekday labors and does not infuse them, Christian life invariably suffers. If Christian theology avoids the topic of work, then it suggests that the bulk of the Christian life—time spent working—is peripheral to the heart of the faith.

This book is suffused with the conviction that Jesus Christ, by the power of the Holy Spirit, redeems, transforms, and takes into the very life of God the ordinary stuff of human life. The most basic claims and symbols of Christian faith relate to the raw materials and practices of human existence: basic foodstuffs that are often hoarded (bread and wine) become, with Christ's blessing, the body and blood of the Savior given for the life of the world; water, which is polluted and wasted, becomes, in Trinitarian grammar, the waters of rebirth and baptism; our bodies, laboring, broken, bruised, objectified, and scarred, are the very body that Jesus assumes in his life and work. Blood, food, baths, bodies: these are the basic themes of human existence that God takes as God's own in Jesus Christ. Might something similar be said of human work? By assuming the flesh, as God works on our behalf in Jesus Christ, are our labors also redeemed, the labors that more often alienate us from one another than unite us? When the shape of human work in the world typically translates into injustice—some work themselves to death while others scrounge for work—Christian hope envisions the transformation of labor. A central claim of this book is that the God of Christian faith *works*: creating, sustaining, redeeming, and making all things new. What is redeemed in Jesus Christ and sanctified by the Holy Spirit elicits our response. Though human work can never detract or add to the work God has already accomplished, it can be an offering for others and for God; when our work draws its life from the triune God, we also contribute to the life of the world.

What, then, is human work? Attempting to define work is as elusive as defining the human person. Most of us have a rather gut-level reaction to work: we know it when we see it. A typical assumption is that work is what persons do for wages: real work is *paid* work. This reduction of labor to pay, however, excludes the vast array of work that is chronically overlooked or deemed secondary by those who write paychecks: caring for children, cleaning house, tending a garden, all the domestic activities that occupy our lives without monetary compensation. In a telling example of how assumptions about work reflect the interests of patriarchy, moreover, those who spend the most time in unpaid work throughout the world are women. Defining work as paid labor ignores much of the world's work and marginalizes millions of workers.

The other danger in equating work with paid labor is that it reflects a capitalist tendency to reduce work to a means of economic exchange. Dorothee Soelle has noted that North Atlantic economies tend to commodify work.[2] Capitalism privileges work's exchange value at the expense of its use value. When work becomes a commodity, it is no surprise that the "real work" of businesspeople, construction workers, and bankers (paid labor) is viewed as more important than the unpaid tasks of cooking, cleaning, and caring for children. However useful and indispensable to human life the latter tasks are, they cannot be reduced to mediums of exchange. And because they are not fungible on the marketplace, they are ignored as work. A Christian theology of work, then, as it reflects the incarnational claim that God takes *all* of human labor as God's own, must expand our understanding of work beyond commodities of exchange.

Some definitions of human work attempt a broader purview by describing work as a "purposeful" activity. Horace Bushnell echoes this broader perspective in his distinction between work and play: "Work is activity *for* an end; play, activity *as* an end."[3] Such definitions, however, risk becoming so broad that they blur the distinctions between work and leisure. Many leisure activities, accordingly, are purposeful: when I go for a hike, for example, my aim is to stretch my legs; to pay attention to trees, birds, streams, and rocks; to inhale the air of the Texas Hill country; to delight in my surroundings and companions on the hike; even to enjoy a laugh and a quickened heartbeat. As much as these hikes involve exercise, however, they do *not* constitute work.

Philosopher and pundit Al Gini has argued for a more restricted definition: work is "that which we are compelled to do by some intrinsic or extrinsic force—the need for money, for self-expression, for accomplishment."[4] His definition is helpful, but can be enhanced by a more explicitly theological account of work given by Richard Higginson, who has suggested that work is "any activity undertaken with a sense of obligation,"[5] to oneself, others, one's community, and God. Higginson's account I find preferable because of its emphasis on obligation rather than compulsion. Work, at least in a theological framework, is characterized not so much by force (in fact, compulsion is part of the sickness of work in workaholic societies), but obligation—connecting and binding oneself to others in a community of laborers.[6] The God who creates the world in love graces us with relationships—to other creatures, to the created order, and to God's very self. God's work of creation elicits our response because God entrusts us with obligations: to attend to the relationships God has provided for us and mend them when they are broken, even if we cannot mend them solely on our own. Work, most comprehensively considered, is the activities we perform, with obligation, for the sake of those relationships, for community.[7]

Christian faith has generally assumed that human persons are made, in part, to work, though work does not constitute the chief end of humanity. Work is one of the activities in which we respond to the God who works on our behalf. In contemporary society, however, most of us work to live: work not only displays a theological response to God's initiative, but the immediate urgency of bodily survival. For an increasing number in American society, this necessity of work translates into compulsion rather than obligation: without work, one quickly falls off the radar screen of society. As we shall see in this study, one of the measures of personhood in American society is whether one is gainfully employed. The vast majority of the working poor, moreover, work long and debilitating hours. Those who work hardest, counter the American mantra, often do not reap tangible benefits.

For many in North America, work is its own reward and a calling: we have found the place where our heart's deep gladness has met the world's deep need.[8] But work also constitutes a problem in North American society. Countless numbers of us are unsatisfied with our work, feel overworked, or are flat out of a job. Work often fails to respond to God's work on our behalf. Work, for too many, has become burdensome and mind-numbing toil. In response to that problem, many of us simply work more while others scramble to find work. For the remainder of the chapter, I survey some of these pathologies of work in a North American context, and how they clash with basic Christian theological claims.

SCARCITY AMID ABUNDANCE: WHO IS WORKING?

Because most people work in North America in order to survive, this survey of working life begins by examining unemployment. Who is working and who is not working for compensation in our heralded economy of growth? Amid boom times and busts, there has never been a time in the American experiment when all adults who desired gainful employment have found it. Though unemployment rates plummeted during the dot-com explosion of the late 1990s, the reality of joblessness has abided throughout cycles of expansion and contraction. The reigning assumption about work in this context is scarcity. As M. Douglas Meeks has written, "Nothing is deeper in the spirit of capitalism, and of socialism as well, than the belief that there is not enough to go around."[9] As resources are finite, so too are the jobs and the work that draw on those resources. Whether societies are conceived along the lines of competitive, tooth-and-nail capitalism or the ownership of means of production by the state, there is never enough work to go around. Joblessness is something to be expected; indeed, a modicum of unemployment is a sign of a healthy economy, as it raises incentives for the jobless to participate more fully in the economic engine that is the United States. This assumption of scarcity should be unsettling to Christians, for it clashes with a bedrock Christian assumption: God's abundant and superfluous giving to creation, which enables us to share out of abundance.

Recent statistics on unemployment in the United States for the 2005 calendar year hover between 5.1 and 5.5 percent.[10] These numbers represent a rather steady decline in the ranks of unemployed since 2003, which have delighted government prognosticators and White House spin-doctors, falling within what many economists call the "natural rate," the level of unemployment that is necessary to ward off inflation and maintain sustainable economic growth.[11] The times, we are told, are good, especially for working Americans. But here the irony is not so subtle: It has become acceptable that some who want work will not work.

Beneath these acceptable numbers, moreover, lurk some alarming levels of unacceptability. Unemployment levels of African Americans, for example, were double that of the population at large over the same time period. Among younger African Americans looking for work, ages sixteen to nineteen, the most recent numbers indicate a staggering 35 percent rate.[12] The relative prosperity of the new millennium, where there seems to be plenty of work to share, disguises the near-permanent joblessness for America's underclass. William Julius Wilson has conducted the most significant studies of how work disappears in impoverished inner cities. These studies reveal that the jobless rate in ten wards of inner-city Chicago's "black belt," for example, is more than 45 percent. His massive study also notes that in the most impoverished areas of the nation's "hundred largest cities, there are ten adults without a job for every six who have one."[13] As work is concentrated in enclaves of prosperity, so, too, is the lack of work in boomtown's barrios. Demographic shifts in the United States, moreover, insulate those who have paid employment from those who do not: prosperous neighborhoods are far removed from ghettoes of urban poverty, if not in mileage then at least in commuting patterns. Urban professionals can speed to work without being bothered by the reality of joblessness, even as freeways bisect once-prosperous but now blighted inner-city neighborhoods. Rarely, in a society where gates, bars, and access codes have become the norms of upwardly mobile living, do the worlds of urban professional and poor intersect. As one competes for jobs in a scarce economy, solidarity with the unemployed gradually slips away. The result, according to Soelle, is that "work becomes a commodity some persons possess and others do not."[14] Work, in a culture of scarcity, is hoarded rather than shared with others.

Official unemployment statistics, however, only include would-be workers who are actively seeking jobs. The U.S. Department of Labor does not include in its monthly prognoses "marginally attached" workers, who want work, and actively sought work during the previous year, but because of family situation, illness, or disillusionment did not seek gainful employment during the four weeks prior to that month's survey. The Labor Department considers these persons to be "discouraged workers," but not among the unemployed. Their numbers, in April 2005 were 1.5 million.[15] Even more significant are those workers who have stopped actively looking for work. These workers, the permanently unemployed, are not even counted by the government. Estimates of their numbers loom large—2.5 million or more[16]—but their omission from statistics is striking. Live without gainful employment long enough, and one does not even count. Accompanying a loss of job is a statistical loss of identity, often mirrored in the psychological loss that one matters less amid the relative prosperity of these boom times.

What do these numbers mean for persons in society—children, spouses, and the elderly—who depend on working Americans for their livelihood? Acceptable levels of unemployment and assumptions of scarcity translate into less-than-abundant life for many American families. "In 2003, 8.1 percent of families in the U.S. had an unemployed member," the third consecutive year that the percentage of families with unemployed workers rose. As with individual unemployment statistics, these numbers increase when one considers the state of Hispanic (11.1 percent) and African American families (13.7 percent).[17] Again, acceptable levels of unemployment translate into unacceptable realities for the dependents of unemployed workers. Turn one's eyes closer to the characteristics of single-parent families, and the statistics are even more glaring. In 2003, families headed by a single mother experienced a 10.2 percent unemployment rate.[18] In one of the most materially prosperous nations the world has ever known, apparently there is not enough work to be shared.

That assumption, which is echoed in the realities of American working life, reflects an economy of scarcity. Few assumptions have achieved such gospel status in neoliberal economics as this one. By and large, it remains unchallenged in public discourse and working practice. Yet it clashes with a fundamental Christian belief: that God creates and redeems out of abundance and invites creation to participate and share in that abundance. Scarcity is antithetical to abundance, and, as Meeks notes, it "may not be made the starting point of a system of economic justice . . . In almost all situations of human life scarcity has been caused by human injustice."[19] As long as scarcity underpins societal attitudes toward work, the work of that society cannot be shared. Instead, one competes for the best jobs and most coveted forms of work. For those who do not succeed in securing desirable work, an ambiguous promise of less-than-fulfilling work is available. Finally, for the losers of the global marketplace, there is the ever-present specter of joblessness.

The divine economy—and apparently the practice of the early Christian church—operates out of a different assumption. In this schema, there is always enough work and grace to be shared. God gives the world all that it needs and works to distribute goods to all creation. The divine life shares with others in giving that spills out for the life of the world.[20] As persons whose lives are taken up, transformed, and consummated in God's very life in Jesus Christ by the power of the Holy Spirit, the church, too, reflects this sharing-in-abundance. What differentiates reigning economic assumptions from their ecclesial counterparts is that sharing in the former is needed as an exigency amid scarcity. In the church's economy, however, the world already has all it needs, and the desire is that *all* should participate in fullness. Hoarding, then, is antithetical to cosmic life in light of God's gift.

We catch glimpses of this sharing-in-abundance in the early chapters of Acts. In sparse prose that has been idealized and romanticized in subsequent generations, Luke writes:

> Awe came upon everyone, because many wonders and signs were being done by the apostles. All who believed were together and had all things in common; they would sell their possessions and goods and distribute the proceeds to all, as any had need. Day by day, as they spent much time together in the temple, they broke bread at home and ate their food with glad and generous hearts, praising God and having the goodwill of all the people. (Acts 2:44–47a)

Those early disciples *worked*: distributing wealth, proclaiming the good news, preparing food, praying, and selling. The new life in Christ did not result in the disappearance of life's labors in a kind of indolent retreat. Instead, *everything* that one had was rendered to the life of the community and given back to God, which was more than enough for life. Work continued, possessions continued, goods were bought and sold, but all of these were shared, not simply for the sake of justice or the interest of fairness. Rather, the followers of the Way shared because God's life invited them into greater fullness. Work continued, but it was transformed from a commodity to be hoarded into a gift to be shared. This sharing of gifts, moreover, resulted in great gladness of heart. Shared work, apparently, does not translate into grudging acceptance of one's fellow workers, but grateful and generous openness to one another. Those traits, to be sure, are marks of good work.

WORKING TO LIVE OR BARELY MAKING A LIVING? POVERTY, WORK, AND THE EUCHARISTIC BANQUET

Another mantra that repeats itself throughout American society is that hard work reaps the rewards of consumer comfort. Work hard, apply yourself, and the good life will be yours as well. So ingrained are these slogans in the collective consciousness that to question them is to court sedition. Hard work drives the miracle that is the American economic machine; we, in turn, celebrate its rags-to-riches beneficiaries: from mythical Horatio Alger to larger-than-life athletes and entrepreneurs. Americans work, so it seems, to live into material abundance. This assumption that we work to live well founders among the millions of Americans who work hard but barely make a living, and it confutes the Christian belief that, regardless of one's working status, there is always room for one more at the Lord's Table. The American mantra, in other words, can little explain the stubborn fact of the working poor. Hard work, for a growing number in society, means little more than an exhausting search for a decent roof for the family and bread to grace the table.

Who are the working poor? In 2003, 12.5 percent of the nation lived at or below the poverty line. One in every five of these individuals were working poor, "those who spent at least 27 weeks in the labor force (working or looking for work), but whose incomes fell below the official poverty threshold."[21] If we consider that many—if not most—of the working poor also care for dependent children or adults, then significantly more than one in five impoverished families qualify as working poor, perhaps as many as four in five. Compounding these statistics is the fact that the number of persons near poverty is 31 percent, which means that the poor *work*, often at more than one job.[22] One of the most difficult myths to dispel in the United States is that the poor are lazy; countless numbers of them work long hours at exhausting jobs for little more than minimum wage. Three in five of the working poor are working full-time.[23]

Focus the lens even more sharply, and the scourge of poverty displays its disproportionate effects. Women who maintain families are twice as likely to number among the working poor than men. A staggering 23 percent of families headed by women with children under the age of eighteen qualified as working poor.[24] Such statistics portray the sordid underbelly of the prosperous economy of the early twenty-first century. Women who work hard are increasingly among the working poor; single women who experience the "second shift"[25] of caring for dependent children are even more likely to be poor. Hard work, in other words, is no guarantee for success; sometimes it barely makes a living. Coupled with these statistics is the reality that percentages of working poor, across nearly all demographic lines, have been increasing with each year since 2000. More and more people who work during these boom times are not partaking in boomtown's benefits.

What are the jobs that promise little more than poverty wages, an absence of job security, and no health insurance? Increasingly, these jobs appear in the service industries: fast-food restaurants, hotels, and big-box emporiums. As

Americans increasingly demand appliances bought at Wal-Mart, devour food at McDonald's, and clamor for lodging at Motel 6, those who purvey these goods upon our demand do not gorge themselves at the buffet of plenty. The logical end of a society that demands the best possible deal are wages—for many—that one cannot live on.[26] Though the percentage of minimum-wage jobs as compared to all wage-earners has steadily declined since 1979,[27] the wage required to qualify as "living" has increased significantly more than the minimum wage. In other words, the gap between the minimum wage and a living wage has steadily increased. Pockets of the nation, furthermore, still lag behind even minimum wage standards. In Texas, for example, 20.7 percent of all wage earners were paid at or below the federal minimum wage of $5.15 per hour, the highest of any state in the union.[28]

As the purchasing power of minimum-wage and middle-income workers has declined, and as the percentage of the working poor has increased, those who have benefited most from the New World Order fall in the upper echelons of American society. Growth in the economy has led to increased profits while the value of worker compensation has actually declined.[29] Prosperity has increased the underclass as it has fattened the coffers of the wealthiest in society. The ratio of CEO pay to the wage of the average worker increased from 24:1 in 1967 to 300:1 in 2000.[30] This disparity resembles more the pattern of plutocracy than democracy; as money translates into political power, many would argue that these statistics represent a betrayal of democracy. Even in the face of increased material abundance, those who work the most desirable jobs have continued to hoard, while many who labor for the CEO barely eke out a living.

If the myth is that we work to live well, and that food always graces the tables of those who work, one Christian counter is that there is always more than enough room at the table for workers and those looking for work alike. Overconfidence in work lurks behind the seemingly innocuous mantra that work makes for a life. The assumption of the eucharistic banquet, however, is different: work is not a prerequisite to the table. Rather, all are welcome, and no matter how many are invited, there is always enough food to go around.[31] Like the servant in the Gospel of Luke who, after gathering the poor, the crippled, the blind, and the lame for a feast, tells his master, "Sir, what you ordered has been done, and there is still room" (Lk. 14:22), at the Lord's Table there is always space for one more. Our lives are possible not because of human work, but by God's grace which nourishes without fail, regardless of how much—or how little—we work. At the Lord's Supper, there are no working poor: all are poor standing in need of God's grace, and all are fed abundantly when bread is broken and wine is poured in Christ's name. Our work, in the end, renders us worthy of none of this abundance.

WE ARE WHAT WE DO:
THE MYTH OF JOB SATISFACTION

In a society such as ours that places a premium on work, it is perhaps inevitable that working individuals—especially in the middle and upper classes—invest so much of their identity in work. Yet another mantra of an industrious society is that "We are what we do." Even dissidents of the industrial age claimed as much. Karl Marx, for example, held a similarly elevated view of human work. By our labors we create ourselves and transform the world: the human person is *homo faber*.[32] If the point of human being is to work, then human persons should find fulfillment in their jobs. Yet the reality of American life betrays disappointing results. Most of us, it seems, are not satisfied with our jobs. We look forward to not working, and in many cases loathe our labors. A society that promises fulfillment in work alone soon proves empty. One theological response to this dilemma is to claim that fulfillment is not found in what we do, but in the knowledge that we belong to God in work and in rest.

How fulfilled is the average American worker? Numerous studies have been conducted over the last decade, most with predictably similar results: Most of us do not experience much on-the-job satisfaction. A 2004 survey by the Conference Board (the promulgators of the Consumer Confidence Index) indicates that about half of us are "content" with our jobs, but only 14 percent are "very satisfied" with them. More glaringly, this same survey claims that a full two-thirds of us are not motivated to meet our employer's goals, and a striking 25 percent of us are merely "showing up for a paycheck."[33] The Dilbert principle of cubicle workers alienated from their employers, chained to mind-numbing bureaucratic tasks, is so humorous to postmodern America because it rings so true.[34]

Though salary can have an impact on job satisfaction, it is not the overriding determinant, as levels of satisfaction have declined across all income levels over the past ten years. A recent study cited in *Psychology Today* notes that the possibility of career advancement, recognition of gifts, and mobility within a particular job plays a greater role than money. According to the researcher Andrew Oswald, professor of economics at the University of Warwick (UK), salary only "minimally influences job happiness."[35] More crucial to satisfaction is the perception that one is not stuck in a job, and will be recognized for one's performance and gifts.

The nadir of job satisfaction, however, appears in the form of occupational stress. In some instances dissatisfaction with work looms so large that work itself becomes a health hazard. In extreme cases, we can loathe our jobs so much that the stresses of work cause physical symptoms. Occupational stress caused 3,418 illnesses in 1997, resulting in an average of twenty-three days of absence from work. Like the indices for poverty, the effects of occupational stress fall disproportionately on women's shoulders.[36] The second shift of housework after office work, apparently, can result in physical illness. The Japanese have a word, *karoshi*, which can be translated as "death from over-work,"[37] and stories that attest to its truth. Though we have not incorporated this term into our national parlance, its resonance is strong among those who have experienced inordinate job stress for too many hours. Work, at its worst, can be a health hazard.

When work becomes its own burden, when satisfaction disappears amid the drudgery of daily tasks, when health itself is endangered, work fails in its promise that we will become what we do. Or perhaps it confirms it as the American nightmare. Work that becomes drudgery and the source of dissat-isfaction is what Marx called alienated labor: "What, then, constitutes the alienation of labor? First, the fact that labor is *external* to the worker, i.e., it does not belong to his essential being; that in his work, therefore, he does not affirm himself but denies himself, does not feel content but unhappy, does not develop freely his physical and mental energy but mortifies his body and ruins his mind."[38] Though many of us are satisfied in our work, for increasing numbers of Americans, alienation is as much a reality as it was for nineteenth-century English coal miners.

When work fails its promise, when the desire to become what we do results in alienation rather than satisfaction, it is helpful to recall the Christian con-viction that we can never be reduced to our individual labors. The true source of our identity is not our job, but the God who adopts us as children in Christ's name. We do not create ourselves in work. God has already created us in love; our work is—in part—a response to God's creative love. We are not who we are because of what we do, but because of *whose* we are. Identity is not created by our labors, but given by the God who works in Jesus Christ on behalf of creation: "I do not call you servants any longer, because the ser-vant does not know what the master is doing; but I have called you friends, because I have made known to you everything that I have heard from my Father" (John 15:15).

HOW MUCH IS ENOUGH?
OVERWORKED AND WORKING MORE

If the elusive promise of American consumerism is that work makes us free,[39] or at least free enough to consume and find an identity, the result will be that we work more. However empty the promise, this prediction has proven true. Amer-icans are working longer, it seems, than at nearly any point in their history, as if we cannot work enough. A theology of work, by contrast, claims that there is such a thing as enough work, because God already works for us.

How much do Americans work? Studies abound, but each confirms that we are working more than ever. The United Nations' International Labor Organization conducted a study in 2001, which determined that Americans worked an average of 1,978 hours in the previous year, a climb over the last study in 1990. These figures put us on the job for 100 hours more than the average Australian, Canadian, Japanese, and Mexican worker. Only workers in South Korea and the Czech Republic logged more hours than the typical American.[40] Behind these averages lurk more sobering statistics. Some studies suggest that 85 percent of us work more than 45 hours per week, and that given the steady increase in time spent on the job since the dawn of labor-saving technologies, most of us can expect to track 58 hours per week on the job by 2010.[41] The oddity of technological advances in each generation (internal combustion engine, electrical appliances, computer, and e-mail) has been that the very devices designed, at least in part, to reduce human labor have actually created more work! We, too, have responded with gusto. In order to cram in the extra hours and squeeze time together with family, 40 percent of us work late, or on weekends, or both.[42] Annual family hours on the job have increased 11 percent since 1975.[43] The time bind is an ever-present reality for American workers, and we have responded simply by piling on more hours at the job. Small wonder that two-thirds of Americans feel overworked.[44]

One of the comforting myths of (post)modern, urban existence is that the further one reaches into the mythic past, the longer people toiled for their daily bread. Progress, the story goes, has ensured less work. But history disrupts these myths. Classical Rome, for example, allowed for ample leisure amid plentiful public festival days. In the middle of the fourth century, 175 days of the calendar year were designated as off-limits for work, with the result that the average Roman worker spent fewer than one-third of their waking hours at work.[45] Even in the oft-lamented Dark Ages, days of leisure were ensured by the church's appointment of fast and feast-days. Juliet Schor estimates that in medieval Europe, the average peasant worked between 120 and 180 days per year.[46] The frenzy of industrialization soon woke us out of these leisurely slumbers. During the heyday of industrialism, working hours had increased 200 to 300 percent since the Middle Ages.[47]

Though hours on the job for the average worker have abated somewhat since the zenith of industrial frenzy (before the advent of labor laws and unions), our hours on the job have steadily increased since mid-century. Much of this increase defies economic necessity. Schor notes that American productivity has increased more than twofold since 1948. Theoretically, then, the average worker could secure the same postwar standard of living at the beginning of the twenty-first century in half the working hours.[48] The problem, of course, is that we have chosen to work more. Why? Part of the answer is that real wages of American workers have not matched increases in productivity.

But another piece of the answer is that the average postwar standard of living was not enough for us: we simply want more. The middle-class home of the 1950s now seems laughably small to the middle class, let alone its lack of two cars and dearth of electronic gadgetry. Americans are now in the enviable position of being among the most productive working societies as well as the most insatiable. Worker productivity in the United States is significantly greater than that of several other postindustrial nations—Japan, the United Kingdom, Canada, Australia, and Spain, for example[49]—but we have chosen to work more in order to consume more things. Consumption has become the stimulus for work: In a society that prizes acquisition, consumption, and disposable commodities, work is not valued in itself, but because work creates the means for devouring more products. More than a half-century ago, Dorothy Sayers observed the waste of the prewar economy in England, with its stress on consumption. Her words are hauntingly relevant today in a North American context: "A society in which consumption has to be artificially stimulated in order to keep production going is a society founded on trash and waste, and such a society is a house built upon sand."[50] The desire to consume more, stimulated by advertising and a glut of cheap goods, paradoxically compels us to work more.

Many of us could consider reducing the hours we work per week, but are reluctant to do so. Consumer cravings, as well as being insatiable, also breed insecurity about the workplace. Rosalind Chait Barnett cites a willingness among male and female workers to decrease work hours, even if it means forgoing pay increases: "In practice, however, few professionals take advantage of the reduced-hours options that are available to them. . . . A major reason for not opting for reduced hours is fear of negative career consequences, a fear that appears to be well grounded."[51] Creature comforts and a higher standard of living are not the only engines driving the American work machine. The more we work, it seems, the more we have become convinced that our work is not enough. Men are particularly prone to this never-ending spiral of believing that one cannot do enough on the job.[52] In order to secure my place at the firm, I need to distinguish myself from my coworkers. Time off can be left to those who do not want to advance. The end result of this cycle, of course, is workaholism: an attitude to work that may have begun innocuously (a tempered sense of pride in one's efforts, a sense of contributing to something worthwhile, a desire to seek new opportunities), but which ends in outright addiction. The workaholic cannot work enough, and like any addict loses her/himself in the addiction. But unlike other forms of addiction in our society, this fix is routinely rewarded by career advancement and the never-ending promise of more money. For a society that can never get enough, we should expect to churn out workers who believe they can never work enough. Work, in this sense, conveys identity. Descartes's mantra appears to have modified somewhat since the Enlightenment. American workers, consciously or not, embody the slogan, "I am busy, therefore I am."

This attitude should ring strange in Christian ears that place hope in the work God is doing on behalf of creation. Because God is at work, we can rest and know that our efforts, as they respond to God's work and are redeemed by Christ, are enough. Christians are reminded of this divine work every time we worship. On the Christian Sabbath, we celebrate not primarily our labors, but the God who has extended grace and freedom to us in Jesus Christ.[53] Liturgy is the "work of the people," but it is also time to rest and trust that God is already at work. This recognition and trust are recorded in Exodus 35–36. After God commands Israel to build a tabernacle suitable for worship of the Lord, the people bring offerings for the tabernacle. In rather painstaking detail, the author records offerings of gold adornment, crimson and purple yarn spun into fabric, stones, gems, spices, and oils brought in response to God's command. Two master craftsmen, Bezalel and Oholiab, inspired with artistry and design, are summoned to "work in gold, silver, and bronze, in cutting stones for setting, and in carving wood, in every kind of craft" (35:32–33) and to teach others these crafts. Other artisans, designers, and embroiderers hear the call—"everyone whose heart was stirred to come to do the work" (36:2)—while the offerings (and the work) keep on coming. Eventually the artisans come to Moses and plea, "The people are bringing much more than enough for doing the work that the LORD has commanded us to do" (v. 5). And, in a response that runs counter to current fixations with work, Moses and others recognize that what the people had already brought "was more than enough to do all the work" (v. 7). When good work is done, the worshipful response is to say that it is enough. Good work, when connected to God's command, does not give birth to a never-ending spiral of labor, but attests to work of the people that is enough in God's sight.

COMMODIFY THIS:
WORK AND HUMAN RELATIONSHIPS

As American workers log increasingly more hours on the job, time spent with their partners, children, and friends slithers away. The reality of home as a place of rest and rejuvenation with the ones we love disappears as workplace demands increase. Arlie Russell Hochschild has well-documented the pattern where "home becomes work and work becomes home."[54] Workplaces are now equipped with the comforts of home—from lounge space to exercise rooms—while incentives to stay longer on the job abound, such as employee-provided childcare. For many, the office is a place, at least, where one does not have to clean up after oneself and the children. One of the rarely acknowledged dangers of a society that works to excess is the gradual commodification of relationships and home. The less time we have with those closest to us, the more—paradoxically—they can become burdens when we finally escape the workplace. When others become objects rather than a summons of love, work has exerted its stranglehold on life. Relationships then become quasi-disposable commodities that I negotiate according to my self-interest. Nothing, it seems, could be further from the Christian claims that others are not burdens, but gifts in God's image; that the most enduring things in the universe are not laboring tasks, but the promise of communion with others.

The massive influx of women in the workplace since the 1960s—at least in white America—has brought about significant changes in domestic life. In Black America, these supposed "shifts" are hardly anything new. Working outside the home has generally been a necessity for women in black communities since the first slave ships landed in the New World. Nonetheless, from 1975 to 2000, the percentage of women working outside the home with children under eighteen rose from 47 to 73 percent, a steep climb indeed.[55] The stay-at-home mother (or father) is now a comparative rarity.

What has resulted, more often than not, for women employed outside the home is the experience of a "second shift" upon returning to the domicile. Employed adult women (regardless of whether they worked full-time or not) spend, on average, an hour more per day than employed adult men cleaning, cooking, and caring for household members. Whereas only 20 percent of men report doing housework on any given day, 55 percent of women do. Likewise, women engage in twice as many hours of child care, regardless of a child's age.[56] The influx of women in the workforce has not led to equal gains, but has resulted in patterns of domestic work that are not shared. Even among married couples who claimed egalitarian relationships—often these were highly educated, urban professionals—the distribution of daily domestic tasks was lopsided solely in favor of a man's rest and a woman's labor.[57] Though Hochschild narrates surprising resilience among harried children and parents, her study also exposes the resentment and annoyance that emerges when couples work too much: wives who resent husbands who don't pull their share, husbands who resent wives for their high expectations, children who internalize squabbles between Mom and Dad. Home has become work for many of us, and the danger is that those who inhabit home with us simply become another object of work.

When relationships become a burden, then households have departed from the gospel promise of communion. At the center of Christian faith is the gift of communion: a divine Son who is the communion of humanity and divinity; a Lord's Supper that is the communion of bread and wine, body and blood; a church that is the communion of God's people; and the promise of eternal life, of our corporate communion with God forever. Relationships matter for Christian faith; indeed, they are what abide in God's good time. One problem of overwork is that it leads us to treat relationships as commodities and burdens. The promise of good work, in responding to the God who creates communion, is that work can be a means of maintaining, rather than destroying communion, so long as we have time to rest.

THE ECLIPSE OF LEISURE
NO SABBATH, NO REST

It is hardly surprising that a society that places a premium on work has a hard time resting. When work becomes its own end, rest becomes superfluous. We then are made for work alone, and can ignore weekends and forgo vacations. Sabbath disappears as a quaint reminder of a more pious time. Yet Christian faith has always claimed that we are made for more than work alone: as God's creatures, we are made for each other and for God. Cultivating these relationships requires time away from work.

Despite a consumer culture bent on selling leisure—witness the advertisements on any given weekend during sports broadcasts—more and more Americans are giving up their hard-earned vacation time. According to a recent article in the *Austin American-Statesman*, more than 30 percent of us do not avail themselves of their full vacation time, while 14 percent do not take any time off for vacation at all. While we are on vacation, moreover, the line between work and leisure is frequently blurred. Thirty-two percent of us, for example, insist on checking e-mail and voice mail while enjoying time off.[58] Compared to other nations, the United States is the only developed nation where law does not mandate minimum vacation time. In other words, if an employer were to decree a no-vacation policy, there would be no recourse for employees to protest. Time off from work in this context is nothing more than a voluntary benefit bestowed by a benevolent employer. Not surprisingly, the United States appears rather vacation-starved compared with other developed nations: Americans average ten to thirteen vacation days per year, compared with Italy's forty-two days, Germany's thirty-five, and "workaholic" Japan's twenty-five.[59]

On those rare occasions when Americans do take time off from work, and when we come home from the office, we increasingly turn to commodified forms of leisure that foster the acquisition of more consumer goods. The Department of Labor's recent time-use study found a single form of leisure that towered above all others: TV watching. It alone accounted for half of the leisure time for both men and women, eclipsing socializing with friends, dining with family, and even spending time with one's spouse or children.[60] Television represents the most passive form of leisure; requiring little expenditure of muscular energy, almost no critical thought, and minimal social interchange, the person who watches is the perfect consumer. He or she simply gorges on information and quasi-entertainment supplied through the channel smorgasbord. Perhaps the quintessential couch potato exercise is no surprise in an overworked society: when time is found away from work, the exhausted worker chooses the least demanding leisure activity of all. But when leisure takes only this passive form, the play of leisure is lost. Play and Sabbath, in the biblical sense, place a premium on the others with whom we journey and call our attention to them.[61] Where TV reigns supreme, time away from work becomes not an opportunity to play with one's fellow creatures, to delight in them simply for who they are, but a time to ignore them. Try asking a simple question to a person engrossed in a television program, and one understands the shortcomings of this form of leisure. The passive TV watcher turns on the set and tunes out the world.

Another form of leisure that has captivated Americans' attention, and which bears a direct correlation to television viewing, is another commodified activity: shopping. Several studies have documented a strong correlation between the number of hours logged in front of the tube and the amount spent on consumer goods. The more we watch, the more we want; the more we want, the more we buy. The sheer volume of advertisements most Americans are exposed to via the air and cable waves is astonishing; over the course of our lifetimes, Americans will spend nearly two years watching commercials. Children are bombarded at even greater levels, ingesting nearly two thousand commercial messages per day, on average.[62] Advertising, in part, is based on the premise of creating desire for products. Observing the behavior of children during and after an hour of watching children's programs on network TV can be especially discouraging. Many of these programs are designed with products in mind: action-toy spin-offs and dolls that correspond to program characters are plugged in the programs themselves and in the commercials that punctuate the program every ten minutes. Cartoon characters that hype sugar-coated cereals and food of questionable nutritional value, as well as cheaply made plastic goodies, become active features of that child's world.

Is it no wonder that shopping has become our second-favorite form of leisure? Malls are not only the new town commons, the place where public gathers and politicians campaign, but also the entertainment emporium. Vacation spots near the beach and mountains are now littered with outlet malls, as if the pleasure of swimming in the ocean or hiking an alpine trail were not enough. Leisure has become something that Americans commodify and sell: it helps the economy run, and no better place to keep the machine well-oiled than at the local mall.[63] When leisure is dispensable; when play becomes not a respite from work to help reenergize our labors, but a hindrance to advancing one's work; when the few times that we do take off time from work become opportunities for more consumption, Sabbath disappears.

One response to a workaholic culture is simply to say no. Human beings are neither made for work nor consumption alone. We can neither be reduced to our labors nor to the goods we acquire. As Calvin wrote, "We are not our own. . . . We are God's."[64] Belonging to God summons us to rest in that knowledge while we rest physically from our own labors. The biblical narratives make this connection explicitly, as Sabbath is bound up with God's very life and the life God bestows on creation. The God who labors for us is also the God who rests on the seventh day, a God who invites and even commands us to rest and worship. Sabbath is indispensable for the divine life and our own. It is not simply a requirement for humans to uphold, but a key to abundant life: "The sabbath was made for humankind, and not humankind for the sabbath" (Mark. 2:27). A Christian theology of work recognizes that sabbath is neither sold nor ignored, but given to humankind for the sake of life itself, that meaningful, worshipful life is found in the interplay of work and rest, giving and receiving. Human beings are both working creatures and Sabbath creatures. As work informs Sabbath, so too does Sabbath infuse work.

CONCLUSION

The preceding survey is not meant to supply an exhaustive study of the shape of work in North America. Indeed, any individual worker will find exceptions to the patterns charted above. Countless workers in our workaholic society have found work that is fulfilling and humane, vocations that offer a balance between labor and rest. Work, for many, can be fulfilling without being the only source of fulfillment. But in many respects, work has failed many of its promises at the dawn of the new millennium. In the United States we have become hardened to the assumption that some must be permanently unemployed; we have acquiesced to the fact that many who work the hardest at menial jobs cannot earn a living wage for themselves or their families; we have sought satisfaction in hard work only to find that promise so empty that we loathe our jobs; we work, by most accounts, too much and take too little time off. And in the wake of this culture of work, many relationships suffer, while we simply desire and consume ever more disposable products.

The second creation story in Genesis suggests that work is not a result of the fall. God forms Adam out of the soil, in part, because there is "no one to till the ground" (Gen. 2:5). Work is given to human beings as part of the abundant life of the garden. Human beings are working beings. But work, according to that same narrative, quickly becomes toil. Labors fail, human beings substitute a good of creation for God's goodness, and the ruptures that infest relationships commence. Work fails in a culture that attributes too much or too little value to it. When work fails, what resources can Christian traditions provide that envision work's transformation? Is fallen work capable of being redeemed? The following chapter turns to those questions by surveying the rich and sometimes conflicting attitudes toward work that Christians have displayed throughout the centuries. Each suggests, in its own way, that nothing—even fallen work—is beyond the scope of God's redemptive activity.

2

Redeemed and Unredeemed Work

Images of Human Labor in Christian Traditions

For centuries Christian faith has assumed that work is necessary for human life. Whether broached in language of vocation, obligation, command, or justice and the common good, varied Christian traditions have claimed that there is such a thing as good work. Though most of these traditions avoid the facile reduction of human persons to their labors (I am my work), they rarely glimpse humanity apart from work. The lexicon of Christian theology, indeed, is permeated by images of human and divine labor: creating, redeeming, making covenant, calling, sending, forgiving, peacemaking, and reconciling. Work has value in these traditions: as God works on behalf of creation, ruling and redeeming the cosmos, human persons are called by God to respond faithfully with their lives and their work. At the far horizon of Christian hope, moreover, God transforms and reorients our lives so that they, too, might dimly reflect the divine life. Work does not disappear in Christian eschatology, but is redeemed and renewed in God's very life.

At the same time, Christian traditions highlight the ambiguity of human work. The workers God calls are the same workers who stop their ears to the divine summons. If Christian faith emphasizes work's value, it underscores work's insufficiency as well. Human work neither saves nor provides ultimate fulfillment. Work on behalf of God's reign can easily be twisted into labor for one's own self-justification and privilege. When work becomes the chief focus of our lives, work's meaning disappears; furthermore, when we glimpse our work apart from others' work, as if work were a commodity to be hoarded, others become obstacles rather than gifts, or even more disturbingly, they become the *means* for the pursuit of one's "own" work. When work is owned by others, it fails to sustain the common good. Work that maintains covenant with others, because of sin, can rapidly degenerate into exploitation. Christian tradition knows the evils of alienated work rather well, even when it has justified evil work, such as its historical acquiescence to slavery. If human persons are meant to work, our work consistently falls short. Work cannot save, and it often condemns.

The history of Christian attitudes toward work is as varied as nearly any other subject of theological inquiry. Simply put, there is no single attitude toward work in Christian faith, no one pronouncement on work that arises out of the cacophony of labor across the ages. Complicating the issue is the fact that no controversy on work in the early centuries of the church (such as those surrounding Christology and the Trinity) arose that could codify rough consensus. Most attitudes toward work display a tension between work as command and work as a reflection of the fall. Few attitudes toward work understand it only as curse; few as only blessing. The richness of our traditions offers ample resources for recovering a sense of good work. As I argue here, theological conceptions of work that are capable of absorbing *both* the blessing and curse of labor are most adequate to describing work's ambiguity in a fragmented world.

REALISM OF WORK:
THE TENSION OF BIBLICAL NARRATIVES

Biblical narratives overflow with work. Between the opening lines of Genesis, which portray God as worker, and the closing chapter of Revelation, with its vision of a new creation, God labors. One of the distinguishing characteristics of biblical faith is that God does not sit enthroned in heaven removed from work, willing things into existence by divine fiat.[1] Unlike the gods of Greco-Roman mythologies, who absolve themselves of work—dining on nectar and ambrosia in a heaven of rest and contemplation—the God of the Bible works. This God molds humans in God's image, establishes covenant with a displaced people, laments when covenant is broken, strives to reestablish covenant with that people, and becomes incarnate to labor, suffer, die, and be raised for the whole world. In its varied trajectories, the Bible takes pains to demonstrate that God's purposes are not achieved automatically and effortlessly. God's work is the labor of extending grace to all creation, work that gives creation all that it needs. As the psalmist writes, "By your strength you established the mountains. . . . You silence the roaring of the seas. . . . You visit the earth and water it, you greatly enrich it. . . . You provide the people with grain, for so you have prepared it" (Ps. 65:6–9). God works to achieve God's purposes in creation, yet we respond to these labors by refusing to accept God's work. The tension of biblical narratives is this: God's work is good for all and enough for all, summoning our work to follow its rhythms; yet we reject God's work, and as a result our labors become toil and drudgery. Though what follows is far from an exhaustive study of biblical attitudes toward work, their varied voices portray human work with uncanny realism.

M. Douglas Meeks notes that the Bible assumes the perspective of the worker—not the master, not the idle person, not the owner of work.[2] Amid its competing trajectories, the Bible values work and people who work. In its opening pages, Genesis portrays God as the worker who speaks, breathes, and molds creation into existence. God's work is the source of all that is. One dimension of our place in the world, accordingly, is to take part in work. Both creation stories in Genesis point to the significance of human work, not as a curse, but as a response to God. In the second narrative, God entrusts Adam with care of the land: "The LORD God took the man and put him in the garden of Eden to till it and keep it" (Gen. 2:15). Work arises not because of the fall, but because the land yields fruit to the industry of human labor. As the narrative begins, work binds creatures together in God's world rather than sets them apart from each other. Tilling the soil fosters our dependence on earth, water, and sun. Keeping the garden encourages mindfulness of all God's creatures. Work, thus glimpsed, is not punishment, but a response to maintain community and well-being in light of God's work of creation and redemption.

Torah recognizes these communal dimensions of work. If the human person is summoned to work in response to God, then covenant sets the parameters for good work. Tending the soil does not mean that workers extract as much fruit or profit from the land as they possibly can. The commands for these gardeners are specific: "When you reap the harvest of your land, you shall not reap to the very edges of your field, or gather the gleanings of your harvest. You shall not strip your vineyard bare, or gather the fallen grapes of your vineyard; you shall leave them for the poor and the alien: I am the LORD your God" (Lev. 19:9–10). Torah protects the land and the vulnerable who inhabit it from profiteering and greed. Work is not to be hoarded or extracted at others' expense, but given for others, for God, for the health of the land. Demanding every last drop of work jeopardizes the land and those most likely to be work's victims. Torah thus recognizes overwork and sets limits to work so that others might live.

Rest, accordingly, accompanies good work. As God rested on the seventh day, so too are creatures in God's image made to rest in the results of work not our own: prayer, contemplation, and leisure reorient life. Sabbath prevents work from becoming endless drudgery while it cultivates mindfulness of God's work. By keeping Sabbath, the day set aside as holy and reserved for not working, we affirm that our labors do not save us. Sabbath, too, warns against overwork: on the seventh day, God's people rest; every seven years the land receives a Sabbath (Exod. 23:10–11); every fifty years, moreover, Israel celebrates the Jubilee, where the land is not worked, where persons return to property they have lost through work, where servants are set free and debts are cancelled. Jubilee sets strict limits to work and the profits of work. "And you shall hallow the fiftieth year and you shall proclaim liberty throughout the land to all its inhabitants. It shall be a jubilee for you: you shall return, every one of you, to your property and every one of you to your family" (Lev. 25:10). Fruits of work gained at the expense of others are to be returned to their previous and hence rightful owners. Jubilee disrupts patterns of work that degenerate into pursuit of riches. When work breaks backs and ruptures relations, when work becomes a commodity to be traded or enslaved, Jubilee mends those broken relationships. Rest from work—for a year—shows that we are not made for work alone.

Torah emphasizes the need for Jubilee, because labor and work are prone to failure. In realities that hauntingly echo our current global economy, Jubilee calls Israel to account for its abuses of work: Land promised to all increasingly fell into the hands of the rich. Israelites made for freedom became indentured to one another. Debt grew at rates that many could not afford. Acquisitive work may have benefited some, but it bred enormous damage to others' lives and land. Jubilee points to the restoration of the wrongs that the prophets routinely lament. When Amos claims, "Because you trample on the poor and take from them levies of grain, you have built houses of hewn stone, but you shall not live in them; you have planted pleasant vineyards, but you shall not drink their wine" (Amos 5:11), he castigates those who extract too much work from others. To own the work of the poor is to break covenant. The way work is practiced, distributed, and shared is a reflection of Israel's claim or rejection of its covenantal promises.

When Jubilee promises restoration, the forgiveness of debt, and return to family land, it echoes the prophets' vision for redeemed work. The New Jerusalem does not offer freedom from work, but freedom in work, where one enjoys the fruits of labor and just compensation. Zechariah admonishes the people to "let your hands be strong," an obvious allusion to manual labor: "For before those days there were no wages for people or for animals. . . . But now I will not deal with the remnant of the people as in the former days, says the LORD of hosts. For there shall be a sowing of peace; the vine shall yield its fruit, the ground shall give its produce, and the skies shall give their dew; and I will cause the remnant of this people to possess all these things" (Zech. 8:10–12). Work does not cease in Zechariah's vision, but reflects the abundance given in God's work. Nowhere in the prophetic literature does the restoration of Zion evoke images of endless laziness or rollicking escape from work. Restoration, rather, is to redeemed work, where the poor are no longer victimized by work.

Similar attitudes and practices of work—its blessing and ambiguity—are found in the New Testament. Jesus castigates those who work at the expense of others in ways analogous to the prophets (Luke 6:24–25; 11:46–47). His parables of God's reign, moreover, assume a worker's context and experience (Matt. 13:3–8; 13:33; Luke 15:3–7). Yet the Gospels often portray Christ's work as it disrupts human labor. Jesus' calling of the first disciples in the synoptics occurs when he accosts unsuspecting fishermen in the midst of their trade. Luke's narrative contains an anecdote not mentioned in Matthew and Mark: After a frustrating night of catching nothing, Jesus suggests that they cast their nets into deeper water. The results are stunning: "When they had done this, they caught so many fish that their nets were beginning to break" (Luke 5:6), as if the encounter with Jesus yields unprecedented bounty in work. Yet Luke refuses to correlate the calling of the disciples with a gospel of prosperity. In the face of an unparalleled harvest, Simon, James, and John leave everything to follow Jesus (v. 11),[3] abandoning their previous work for a different kind of labor. Trades here are relativized; their value is found neither in results nor their permanence. Rather, work changes—often quite dramatically—as one is drawn toward the work of Jesus.

The value of work in some of Jesus' parables, like the calling of disciples away from work, represents an alternative to the assumption that those who work hardest, longest, or in the most respected professions deserve the most. The parable of the laborers in the vineyard, for example, includes the odd practice of a landowner paying the same daily wage to workers regardless of whether they started working in the morning or late afternoon. Those who want to work, whom no one would hire, are rewarded as if they had completed a full day's work (Matt. 20:1–16). In a society such as ours (and perhaps that of the ancient Near East) that assumes that some levels of unemployment are acceptable and that the wages for those looking for work must be kept low to ensure motivation as one climbs the ladder of success, this parable is disruptive. The value of work is not its result or the length of time one has been engaged in work; rather, its value is that *people* are doing the work. In the upside-down values of the reign of God, those without paid work are valued as much as those who begin work at the crack of dawn.

These alternative practices of the upside-down reign do not assume that persons will cease working. Indeed, the vibrancy of early church life contains startling combinations of work: some of the saints, like the disciples, abandon their previous labors for missionary activity, others share work in common (Acts 2:44–45), and some remain in so-called secular vocations, such as Lydia, the dealer of purple cloth (Acts 16:14). Even Paul does not abandon his trade of tentmaking in the midst of his missionary journeys (Acts 18:3). Many tasks, it seems, can reflect the reign of God. In Christ, work is valued because the doers of work belong to Christ.

Even the far horizon of hope in the Bible does not suppose that labor vanishes in God's reign, but will be renewed by divine work. The restoration of Jerusalem in Isaiah contains the injunction for its people to "build up, build up the highway, clear it of stones, lift up an ensign over the peoples" (Isa. 62:10). Here the work of the people is a response to what God has already done. The Bible itself ends with a cosmic vision of this restored Zion. The central metaphor for Christian hope in the Book of Revelation is not a lazy pastoral scene, but a renewed city: a place of human work, built by human hands, restored and reclaimed by God's work. When the author of Revelation proclaims that people will bring to the New Jerusalem "the glory and the honor of the nations" (Rev. 21:26), one implication is that work continues in Zion.

No single attitude about work dominates biblical witness other than the seemingly mundane fact that the Bible assumes the perspective of workers. But this perspective, in itself, is significant. As the Bible surveys work's pain and travail, its joy and blessing, its indispensability for faith and its tendency to obstruct the call to discipleship, it assumes that work is more than something to occupy idle time. As taken, claimed, and blessed by God, work has value, even in its ambiguity. Perhaps the book of the Bible that best captures the tension is Ecclesiastes. In stark realism, Qoheleth describes the pain of work as toil, "vanity and a chasing after wind" (Eccl. 2:11). Qoheleth dashes any presumption or overwrought pride in our labors. No work that is human work endures; all that can be gained from work eventually disappears. The questions the Preacher poses are blunt: "What do people gain from all the toil at which they toil under the sun?" (1:3). The short answer is nothing, at least nothing that endures.

The problem, of course, is that we turn our eyes from this stubborn fact. We want to believe that our work endures. But as soon as we fixate on work's legacy and endurance, we chain ourselves to an endless treadmill. The more we attach ourselves to work, the more we assert its independent value and endurance, the less satisfied we become with the results and process of work. In language strikingly similar to current discussions of work and addiction, Qoheleth claims "All human toil is for the mouth, yet the appetite is not satisfied" (6:7). When we pin ultimate value and fulfillment to work or the results of work, we become insatiable and bind ourselves to work that does not endure. Insatiability, in turn, results in misery and despair. Qoheleth muses, "So I hated life, because what is done under the sun was grievous to me; for all is vanity and a chasing after wind" (2:17). Cursed by work we cannot shed, we wind up despising life itself.

Were Ecclesiastes to leave the reader with these impressions alone, the meaning of work would appear empty. Qoheleth avoids nihilism, however, by pointing to the work that abides and gives meaning: God's work. The only lasting value of work is in the fact that *God* gives us work: "I know that there is nothing better for them than to be happy and enjoy themselves as long as they live; moreover, it is God's gift that all should eat and drink and take pleasure in all their toil. I know that whatever God does endures forever; nothing can be added to it, nor anything taken from it" (3:12–14). This recognition is both humbling and liberating: it requires modesty for those of us accustomed to placing an ultimate sense of identity in work, and it frees us from the insatiable search of finding our chief meaning in work. We are not what we do for a living; we are children of God. Work has meaning because it comes from God and is directed back to God. In the meantime, we are to enjoy our companions as we work and play, eat and drink. By claiming repeatedly that there is nothing better for humans than to enjoy toil, Qoheleth neither glorifies nor denigrates work, but glimpses it as one component of earthly life. In this regard, Ecclesiastes echoes much of the Bible's tendency to avoid assigning too little or too much meaning to our work in response to God. Work, like everything else in human life, is claimed and blessed by God, molded anew by God's work.

WORK AS CURSE

If biblical narratives stress the renewal of work, they also point to work's burden. In a broken world, work is more often curse than blessing. Whether epitomized by the chains of slavery, the struggle for a living wage, or the experience of having one's work owned by another, our labors often alienate us from one another and ourselves. Work can grind down, humiliate, and exhaust workers. In a global economy, moreover, alienated work can lead to material prosperity for a chosen few. Wealth that feeds on demeaning labor has many faces: cheap jeans worn in midwestern suburbia sewn with child labor in the third world, defense contracting booms in California that produce carnage on continents far from the Golden State. The middle classes in the United States also experience alienation of their own. Considering how much late-night comedy and popular music satirizes work—"Take This Job and Shove It"—we often long to flee our jobs. American leisure fantasies, no doubt, are fueled in part by persons who hate their work. Thank God it's Friday.

Biblical traditions are aware of this strand of the human condition. Almost as soon as God entrusts human persons with tilling the soil, they experience work as backbreaking toil. Expulsion from the garden results in a lifetime of hard work. If Eden promises fruitful abundance, life beyond the garden brings thorns, thistles, and an intensification of labor: "By the sweat of your face you shall eat bread" (Gen. 3:19a).[4] The trajectory of the narrative indicates that work can breed its own frustration, exhaustion, and despair. In vivid imagery, Genesis captures the all-too-familiar experience that work is its own kind of torture and can even breed violence, as the subsequent narrative of Cain and Abel demonstrates.

The central narrative of the Pentateuch—the Exodus—best captures the violent alienation of work. The story of God's covenant with Israel begins with stark descriptions of alienating work, as Israel is enslaved in Pharaoh's land. In Egypt, Israel knows work as an assault on personhood, as the Israelites are owned by others. These owners demanded work regardless of its costs to the worker. The writers of Exodus do not mince words: "The Egyptians became ruthless in imposing tasks on the Israelites, and made their lives bitter with hard service in mortar and brick and in every kind of field labor. They were ruthless in all the tasks that they imposed on them" (Exod. 1:13–14). As the story of covenant begins, Israel experiences work as violence. They labor at mortar and brick so that others may benefit from the edifices they construct, that others may eat the fruit of the fields. In Egypt, Israel does not own its work; it is owned by others who wield power with the sword.

As Israel chafes under its yoke, the taskmasters impose even greater burdens. In a decree that makes no sense other than to further humiliate workers, Pharaoh tells the supervisors:

> You shall no longer give the people straw to make bricks, as before; let them go and gather straw for themselves. But you shall require of them the same quantity of bricks as they have made previously; do not diminish it, for they are lazy; that is why they cry, "Let us go and offer sacrifice to our God." Let heavier work be laid on them; then they will labor at it and pay no attention to deceptive words. (5:7–9)

Mistaking religious devotion for laziness, demanding efficiency instead of a humane workplace, Pharaoh anticipates the cry of any manager who places products above people, work over workers. When efficiency rules supreme, workers become disposable annoyances. As God guides the covenant people out of Egypt and into the promised land, Israel journeys from the violent work of slavery into the promise of free work in a land flowing with milk and honey, where Israel will be God's servant. In life and in work, Israel belongs to God.

The past two centuries have witnessed several prophets of work's alienation, the most significant being Karl Marx. For Marx, the promise of work often gets lost amid the grim and grisly accumulation of capital. In his eyes, work is a paramount life expression, the way human persons create and express themselves: work is, of all "forms of society an absolute condition for the existence of humanity," mediating "the metabolism between man and nature, and therefore human life itself."[5] Work makes life possible, but work fails whenever the goal is exchange and profit making. The problem with modern forms of labor is that work becomes a means to profit, typically for someone other than the worker. Miroslav Volf summarizes Marx well: "One precondition of the capitalist mode of production is . . . that the primary goal of production is not the use of products . . . but the exchange of products as commodities. A product that a worker makes has no value for her as a product, but only as a *means* to acquire another needed product or service."[6] In capitalist economies, work becomes less an expression of oneself, less an embodiment of the common good, and more a means of acquisition. This longing for acquisition, in turn, becomes more insatiable with each passing day. Work in this economy places workers in an insoluble dilemma: work is owned by another, for the profit of another; the products of my work are valuable only insofar as they can be exchanged for other products; but workers will never amass the profits necessary for the satisfaction of acquisitive desires. Workers, in short, become alienated from their work: unable to acquire the requisite goods, unable to own the products of their labors. Rather than self-expression, work becomes slavery under a new name.[7]

Speaking in direct opposition to the means of liberation that Marxism announces, Pope Leo XIII echoes Marx in describing the plight of modern workers. His 1891 encyclical, *Rerum Novarum*, has become a classic text in Catholic social ethics, highlighting the curse that work has become for many workers. Leo implicates much in his letter: unchecked competition, "rapacious usury," and "the hiring of labor and the conduct of trade . . . concentrated in the hands of comparatively few." In a manner akin to Pharaoh's Egypt, the very rich "have been able to lay upon the teeming masses of the laboring poor a yoke little better than that of slavery itself."[8] When work is experienced only as a means for fattening others' coffers, when the wages of one's daily labor are less than what is needed to provide for a family,[9] work is alienation.

Rerum Novarum is equally critical of unrestrained capitalism as state-imposed socialism. Both demean workers by placing profit or an elusive collectivism above the value of each person. In unrestrained capitalism, the broader good is the accumulation of wealth; in state collectivism, the broader good is the elimination of private ownership. Both ideologies inhibit human freedom. Where unrestrained capitalism shoves victims of accumulation to the wayside, leaving the mass of workers in chains of poverty, socialism deprives workers of the fruits of labor—private property and workers' connections to family and local communities. Both systems place something else before persons. In 1891, however, the reality of unrestrained capitalism was rending a greater tear in the fabric of life, as large-scale experiments in socialist economies had not yet emerged. Leo's critique, understandably, spends far more time dwelling on the injustice of excessive wealth accumulation. The encyclical employs the language of salvation in rescuing workers from greed: "The first thing of all to secure is to save unfortunate working people from the cruelty of men of greed, who use human beings as mere instruments for money-making. It is neither just nor human so to grind men down with excessive labor as to stupefy their minds and wear out their bodies."[10] A system that places profit ahead of people invariably takes any warm body as a cog in the machine. The logic of unrestrained capital will even employ young children as instruments for the owner, a practice that Leo finds particularly abhorrent, as it erases the possibilities of education, play, and even the future.[11]

The last century has witnessed a continuation of the grim realities that Leo announced. Child labor continues unabated in many corners of the world; the gap between wealthy and poor on a worldwide scale is increasing; third-world nations stagger under the burdens of debilitating debt. Profit, it seems, has become the bottom line in the New World Order. The hyper-specialization of labor in a technological economy, moreover, has rendered workers less satisfied with their own work. Job satisfaction in the United States, for example, seems to be decreasing, as workers become more distanced from the purpose and meaning of their work. The Taylorism of old, which chained workers to endless repetitive tasks on an assembly line in the name of profit, has been replaced by technocratic specialization, so that fewer and fewer workers participate in large-scale planning and vision. Alienation has many faces in the global economy. But in each case, workers become distanced from their labor and its fruits. Christian tradition is no stranger to this recognition. The point of recognizing work as curse, according to Leo, Marx, and others, is not to claim that this is all that work can be, but to lament what has become of work. If work is a curse, it is a curse of our own making and not what God intends for workers.

WORK AS ANTIDOTE TO IDLENESS

If considering work as a curse laments the hell we have made of work, another tradition within Christianity lauds work as a necessary means of preventing even greater disaster. In a fallen world, work becomes an antidote for our tendency to live out of balance. The ascetic view of work is that it restrains the passions, calms unease, and soothes the soul. Most bluntly, work prevents us from getting into further trouble. Throughout every age of the church's history, prominent voices have recognized potential snares to Christian life that are present in the world. One of the chief dangers, potentially lethal to the soul, is idleness. Early monastic movements seized upon idleness as sufficient reason for work's necessity. Yet its trajectory is also glimpsed in modern-day Protestants who view work as a means of restraint. According to this tradition, work is not so much valued for what it is, but for what it prevents: the dissipation of life in laziness.

One classic text that emphasizes the restraining function of work is *The Rule of St. Benedict*, which traces its origin to the sixth century. Though the Benedictines were not the first monastic movement, the *Rule* codified many of the norms for subsequent monastic communities throughout Western Christendom. Among these norms are the exhortations to work and regulate the hours of each day: "Idleness is an enemy of the soul. Therefore, the brothers should be occupied according to schedule in either manual labor or holy reading. These may be arranged as follows: from Easter to October, the brothers shall work at manual labor from Prime until the fourth hour. From then until the sixth hour they should read."[12] In the background of these rules is the conviction that the Christian life must be kept occupied. The Christian life is productive: in work, in prayer, in study. Faced with too little to do or too little to read, our soul becomes imperiled. Even reading sessions, Benedict notes, need supervision by superiors so that "no one is slothful, lazy, or gossiping."[13]

Though Benedict's exhortations may sound at times like warnings to stay busy, work signifies more than an antidote to sloth in the *Rule*. More positively, work is mutual service in Christ's name, the way Christians travel the path of discipleship. In the midst of a chapter on kitchen duty, Benedict writes: "The brothers should wait on one another. . . . After completing his weekly kitchen chores, the monk should clean on Saturday. He must wash the towels the brothers use for drying hands and feet. Everyone's feet are to be washed by the monk finishing his week's service and the one starting his."[14] No task that sustains community is too repugnant for any of its members. Without preparations that allow eating to take place, the community would not survive. As one serves another, so all become servants. The practice of footwashing, which recalls John's narrative of the Last Supper, signifies that the beginning and end of Christian life is service. Small acts of supposedly menial work—washing dishes, cleaning towels, caring for other's feet—are tokens of our participation in Christ's self-giving love.

Six hundred years later, in another manual for monastics, William of St. Thierry offered similar reflections on the nature of work. Claiming that the greatest evil "which can befall the mind is unemployed leisure," William claims that activity should "always leave something in the mind that will contribute to the soul's advancement."[15] Work thus has both a restraining and a productive function—rescuing the soul from idleness, whetting the "taste for spiritual things."[16] For William, work has less intrinsic value than instrumental value. Work is worthy because of the fruits it produces in spiritual life. The relation between physical labor and spiritual benefit is clear: "It is not spiritual exercises that exist for the sake of bodily exercises but bodily for spiritual."[17] The hierarchy of spirit over body is explicit in the *Golden Epistle* and is evident in the hierarchy within work itself. The most valuable work is work that has "greater likeness and kinship to the spiritual; for example, meditating on something to be written or writing something to be read for spiritual edification." By contrast, manual labor in the open air can deplete the spirit and distract the senses.[18] Not all labors are equal: godly work resembles the activities of most Cistercians, while perilous work looked like the labor of those outside the monastery's walls.

This distinction between the "spiritual" work of monastics and the ordinary labor of laypersons crescendos through the high Middle Ages. Whereas Benedict glimpsed an indissoluble connection between manual labor and prayer, by the fourteenth century some monastic movements claimed that "real" work was contemplative instead of active. Movements such as the Carthusians that emphasized withdrawal and seclusion were particularly prone to valuing contemplation over activity. Though the spiritual classics of this period are rarely as crass as to suggest that contemplation is to be valued above all other kinds of work, most writings devoted to contemplatives assume degrees of progress away from the active life into ever-deeper communion with God. Insofar as this progression is offered as a model for the monk's growth, it assumes that pilgrims reflect godly work at the end of the contemplative journey rather than at its beginning, while she or he is immersed in active labors. For many monastics, the story of Mary and Martha (Luke 10:38–42) became an allegory for the contemplative vis-à-vis the active life. According to the author of *The Cloud of Unknowing*, Mary, who sits attentively at Jesus' feet and has "no time for the busy activity of her sister . . . [and] stands for all contemplatives, who should conform their behavior to hers."[19] Martha, meanwhile busied with the work of the house so that the household can show hospitality to the guest, is likewise engaged in holy work: hers are the labors that make contemplation possible. Nonetheless, many contemplatives doubtless took heart in Jesus' response that "Mary has chosen the better part" (v. 42). Though most monastic movements never bifurcated contemplation and labors of service, their mystical edges in the Middle Ages assumed that contemplation was an assured good in itself, regardless of its direct connection to serving one's fellow creatures. Indeed, contemplation became the supreme service to God as the pilgrim journeyed ever deeper into the divine life. Work, accordingly, became a means of restraint in channeling the soul's journey into God.

As much as Protestantism cast aspersions on the separation of labor and contemplation, it emerged with asceticism of its own. Though many of his diagnoses of the Protestant ethic have been disputed, Max Weber's analysis of Calvinism represents an interpretation of work as restraint. According to Weber, Calvinism—particularly in its Puritan manifestations—"works with all its force against the uninhibited *enjoyment* of possessions; it discourages *consumption*, especially the consumption of luxuries."[20] One works not to enjoy the baubles of success or to rollick in wealth, but to restrain oneself through savings and the creation of capital. Work, according to the Protestant ethic, does not possess so much intrinsic value as it is a means of restraining passions and creating wealth for "*practically useful* things"[21] on communal and individual levels. Work thus becomes a necessary means for taming our elemental drives and promoting common good. Work, in other words, is a necessary antidote to sin with admirable social benefits: we are better off working than not. Whether witnessed in monastic guides, mystical texts, or disputed interpretations of Calvinism, work has often exhibited a restraining function in Christian life. Though this ascetic view has strengths of its own, especially as it stresses the service necessary for godly work, the danger of ascetic views alone is that they minimize the intrinsic value of work, the unique gifts of workers, and perhaps even God's calling on human life, regardless of one's station.

WORK AS CALLING AND VOCATION

Throughout his massive corpus, Martin Luther argued vociferously against the devaluation of ordinary labors such as farming, parenting, and cobbling. Monasticism, he claimed, had conceived vocation too narrowly, co-opting the term to speak primarily of church work. His response was to consider all productive work a vocation, so that the labors of the butcher *and* the bishop might be understood as responses to God's claim on human lives. Before he could broaden this sense of call, however, a broadside needed to be fired against restricted understandings of call that demeaned the work of ordinary Christians.

A monk himself, Luther lampoons monastics for embodying the idleness they supposedly combat. In a surprising twist of Benedict's warning, Luther claims that monks in seclusion do not work, even in cases where Christian charity demands it: "A religious is not allowed to leave the monastery, visit the sick, and devote himself to other Christian service. . . . Because manual labor is prohibited, they do no work. They are supported by the rest of the world, devouring everyone else's substance although they are perfectly hale and hearty. This is to the great detriment of the genuinely poor."[22] Monasticism, Luther claimed, absolved monks from working while they ignored the destitute. This lack of work behind cloister walls meant that monastics were dependent on others' work, and hence drained resources from the needy. When fewer people work, there is less bounty to go around. Luther assumes that monastics grow fat on the labors of others: "The religious orders are not supported by their labor. They are like a lazy rogue who does not exert himself bodily but lets others work for him, filling his belly through the sweat and blood of others."[23] Luther argues against monastic work by calling it little more than idleness. In a foreshadowing of later political-economic theories, Luther claims that the leisurely labor of some is sustained by the productive, active work of many, often at the expense of ordinary workers.

Nonetheless, Luther does not attack the necessity of contemplative life. The problem with monasticism is not its stress on contemplation, but its understanding of contemplation removed from the cares and labors of lay workers. Contemplative work—which Luther doubtless embraced in his astonishingly productive written corpus—had to be connected to the struggles and issues of working Christians.[24] When contemplation removes itself from the active life, contemplation disparages ordinary work. As an antidote, Luther uplifted mundane, seemingly unpleasant labors as marks of Christian service and response to God. One of his most colorful examples was the work of diaper changing: "When a father goes ahead and washes diapers or performs some other mean task for a child . . . God, with all his angels and creatures, is smiling—not because that father is washing diapers, but because he is doing so in Christian faith."[25] Though acts of child care have value for Luther in themselves, they also become a response to God's call on life when carried out in faith. In this regard, *all* labors for others, no matter how small or insignificant, are vocations.

Luther's articulation of vocation exhibits simultaneously revolutionary and conservative consequences. On the one hand, naming all forms of human work vocation (with the exception of work destructive to human society, such as crime and prostitution) implies a spiritual egalitarianism that deems work honorable in God's sight. God calls each one of us to labor, and we respond in labors uniquely our own. The value of work stems from a divine call that binds us in mutual service. No one form of work is more worthy than another, since God summons us to all vocations. In this regard, Luther levels the distinctions of value between "active" and "contemplative" life. He recognizes that his labors as a scholar are dependent on the work of the butcher, baker, and candlestick maker.

On the other hand, Luther's understanding of God's call betrays a wooden view of the social order. God summons persons to labors and stations in life that they occupy their entire lives:

> God assigns to each man his toil in accordance with his powers and in
> keeping with his calling. . . . To each one God has assigned his por-
> tion. . . . [God] wants you to do your duty happily in accordance with
> your assigned task and leave other things to other people. . . . You
> should, he says, have a happy spirit and an active body, but in such a
> way that you abide in *your assigned place*.[26]

The language of vocation that proved revolutionary for the priesthood of all
believers also reflected dominant assumptions about social ordering. If God
called all to stations and vocations, rarely did God call persons to move out of
their assigned place. Once called to be a peasant, peasants were to remain in
that station for life.[27]

John Calvin echoes Luther's conception of vocation and extends it not only
to one's means of livelihood, but to all actions that occupy human existence.
Our duties, Calvin claims, are not restricted to work, but encompass every
dimension of life. He writes, "The Lord bids each one of us in all life's actions
to look to his calling."[28] Like Luther, Calvin assumes that our unique callings
impose limits to our sphere that cannot be transgressed. The language of vocation, in his sight, preserves order as much as it liberates persons from all walks
of life to see their work as a response to God's word. Indeed, Calvin juxtaposes
lowly occupations with God's calling: "No task will be so sordid and base, provided you obey your calling in it, that it will not shine and be reckoned very
precious in God's sight."[29] The primary value of our labors is not the work
itself, but the One who calls us to labor. Work is precious because God summons us to work.

Luther and Calvin are cautious about assigning too much significance to work.
Our labors, no matter how noble, neither save us nor reckon us righteous. Indeed,
Calvin seems dour about the possibility of good work. Because everything that
human persons do is tainted by the scourge of sin, labors of charity, he notes,
often belie selfish motives and deceitful ambition. "The best work that can be
brought forward from [believers] is still always spotted and corrupted with some
impurity of the flesh, and has, so to speak, some dregs mixed with it."[30] Most of
our work—if not all of it—is ambiguous at best. The Reformers' continued
emphasis on justification by grace through faith, not works, is a continual
reminder of work's ambiguity: "Faith righteousness so differs from works righteousness that when one is established the other has to be overthrown."[31] From
the Reformers' perspective, we tend to attribute too much value to our work, as
if our occupations and actions render us righteous in God's sight. The effects of
this overestimation of ourselves are disastrous: because our work always falls
short, the more we attribute value to it, the more we crowd out the work of
Christ, whose work is the only saving labor. In truth, our work convicts us; the
only remedy is to attribute all righteousness to Christ and none to our labors.

If these polemics on works righteousness are the Reformation check against workaholism and pride in our labors, the Reformers recognized the value of obedient work. When God calls each person uniquely, our response in carrying out that call indicates the righteousness that belongs to God alone. Work, as vocation, is fulfilling not because it enriches oneself (though it may), but because of its obedient response to the creator. The value of vocation is not self-referential, but in rendering one's work to God, in all components of one's life.

Recalling these voices from the Reformation, a flurry of recent writings in North America also focus on work as vocation. In an era during which many seem dissatisfied with their work, where many persons experience the disconnect between worship on Sunday morning and one's life during the other six days of the week, reclaiming language of vocation can bring spiritual vigor to physically and mentally depleted labors. One of the most significant rearticulations of vocation is found in Parker Palmer's *Let Your Life Speak*. Deeply rooted in Quaker traditions, Palmer offers a critique of the heteronomy that lingers in Luther and Calvin: Vocation is not a "goal to be achieved but as a gift to be received . . . Vocation does not come from a voice 'out there' calling me to become something I am not. It comes from a voice 'in here' calling me to be the person I was born to be, to fulfill the original selfhood given me at birth by God."[32] For Palmer, discerning one's vocation can be painful; distinguishing the inner voice from the din of expectations and competing values in the maddening crowd takes time and effort. Finding one's vocation, however, is joyous, and occurs where the heart's deep gladness meets the world's deep need (Buechner). Palmer's inward turn—discerning vocation in oneself as it discovers God's claim and call—thus throws persons out into wider communities of concern and work. As it critiques the emphasis on the external voice of call in Luther and Calvin, it recalls their focus on the original gift of vocation and work.

In a slightly different vein, Douglas Schuurman's recent articulation of vocation offers a critique of the reduction of vocation to paid work. The problem with current church discussions, he claims, is that vocation assumes a narrow context: "Constructive treatments of vocation for the past few decades constrict the idea to paid work, neglecting the potential of vocation to integrate paid and unpaid work, domestic and 'public' life, church and world, personal identity and varied roles, faith and life."[33] For Schuurman, the Reformation meaning of vocation is more expansive than work and job. To counteract this reductionism, Schuurman distinguishes the primary calling of all Christians from multiple particular callings unique to each individual. "The primary Christian calling is to love God with all one's heart, soul, strength, and mind, and to love one's neighbor as oneself."[34] The love commandment, obviously, encompasses more than one's paid work; it forms the fabric of one's entire life as a response to God. Yet the general commandment to love seems abstract without the particular callings that claim each person. I carry out that commandment in the various callings that shape my life: in work, relationships, leisure, family, and community. I love neighbor and God, in other words, *as* teacher, friend, parent, spouse, citizen. For Schuurman, particular callings—which are always multiple—make the love commandment concrete. The strength of Schuurman's position is that it is more elastic than most Reformation articulations. In his understanding, we are always more than our work. Our labors, moreover, may change over time as we discern God's summons on our entire lives.

The language of vocation has exhibited surprising endurance throughout the last several hundred years, and is currently experiencing a renaissance.[35] In the Reformation era, recovering language of vocation for all workers disrupted the tendency to value "sacred" over "secular" work. The wisdom of vocation is its grounding of human work in the redeeming grace of God, and its insistence that our primary vocation is always more than our particular job. At the same time, however, the language may exhibit socially conservative tendencies that encourage one to stay in one's place.[36] If we are to claim that God calls persons uniquely, then we must also recognize that the human propensity for order may obstruct the *transformative* call of God's grace.

WORK AS SALVATION

While the language of vocation deems work a response to God's call, the language of fulfillment considers work as an expression of salvation. Though this optimistic attitude about work has tentative roots in antiquity, in the West it emerged primarily in the wake of the Enlightenment. As humanity threw off the chains of arbitrary authorities—ecclesial, political, and social—persons could reinvent themselves through work. If one human problem was alienating and unfulfilling work, much of the solution lay in work's transformation. Voices in this strain often do not make overt theological claims, but invoke a loose religious vocabulary in describing the aim and ends of work. Good work makes us free, by expressing who we are. Through these rosy lenses, work achieves apotheosis.

The political writings of G. W. F. Hegel betray this sanguine attitude to human labor. A quintessential philosopher of freedom, Hegel observed that human work degenerated to toil under the burden of alien authorities. When work is demanded from us by others, when it is a response to force rather than creativity, work enslaves.[37] The dynamic of Spirit let loose in the world, however, will not rest in alienation. Spirit seeks expression, in part, through the work of our hands and minds. "As the individual in his *individual* work already *unconsciously* performs a *universal* work, so again he also performs the universal work as his *conscious* object; the whole becomes, as *a* whole, his own work, for which he sacrifices himself and precisely in so doing receives back from it his own self."[38] The journey to meaningful work is nothing less than a journey out of slavery into freedom. Recalling imagery from the Exodus, Hegel suggests that properly oriented work can make us free.

Karl Marx seizes Hegel's understanding of free, creative work and spins it in a more overtly economic direction. For Marx, proper work is not only a means to freedom, but the center of human life itself. We are made to work; work results in "self-realization" and therefore "real freedom."[39] We work not because we have to, but because our deepest desire is to create through work. Humanity builds itself, inventing itself and the world through its labor. Like Hegel, Marx claims that the work of the masses does not constitute creative work. When workers do not own the means of production, labor becomes an extraction from workers rather than an expression of oneself. Modern capitalism thus is an enslaving system for workers, which can be overcome only through collective ownership of the means of production. When workers own their work and the means of work, their work, too, will make them free.[40]

Two critiques of this vision of work are relevant for Christian theology. In the first place, seeing work as salvific recalls a works righteousness that most strands of the tradition would reject. For Marx, this is especially the case. The solution, as Marx puts it, is part of the problem that Christian faith diagnoses: we often attribute too much value to work, as if work alone could save us. To value work need not assume that human beings find salvation in work. Only God's grace saves; our work is a response to that grace, not a means of receiving grace. A second, related critique is that overly sanguine views of work may promote the reduction of persons to their work. If the essence of personhood is to work, then the danger is that we become our work, and hence incapable of rest, worship, and play. Christian theology, at its best, resists reductionism: the person is always more than what she produces or how he labors. Workers or not, we are children of God, made for relationship with God, creation, and each other. If work is a dimension of those relationships, it does not exhaust their vast riches.

WORK AS COCREATIVE

If salvation overestimates work, recent theological attempts to recover the dignity and value of labor have become popular in the past three decades by claiming human work as cocreative with God. This slogan of cocreativity has gained wide credence in surprisingly diverse quarters: the encyclicals of Pope

John Paul II, the writings of Episcopal philosopher/priest Armand Larive, and the theology of Miroslav Volf. In these readings, meaningful work is grounded in God's extension of grace to all creation.

John Paul II extols work for its capacity to transform the world. Human persons are unique, in part, because their work molds, shapes, and builds new things. In world construction, "man . . . *achieves fulfillment* as a human being and indeed, in a sense, becomes 'more a human being.' "[41] John Paul II interprets Genesis 1 to mean that work in the image of God corresponds to subduing and dominating the earth.[42] God intends for us to work—work that is endowed with enormously creative and destructive capacities.

Created in God's image, human persons can work in ways that preserve their dignity as workers or in ways that promote suffering and toil. Despite work's ambiguity, the creativity and ingenuity of work contribute something to creation. God summons human workers to take part in the redemption of the world. The religious valuing of labor here is unmistakable, even when work seems a burden. "This work of salvation came about through suffering and death on a Cross. By enduring the toil of work in union with Christ crucified for us, man in a way collaborates with the Son of God for the redemption of humanity."[43] Good work, we should expect, will bring its own challenges and pain. For John Paul II, this is not masochism, but the conforming of human labor to the life and work of Christ. Good and godly work is cruciform, recalling the creativity and sacrifice of the Savior. When our work honors persons in constructing something new, we participate in the redemption of the world.

Armand Larive's recent book *After Sunday* echoes *Laborem Exercens* as it considers "that the work of humanity is cocreative and finds its meaning by accompanying the creative work of God."[44] Larive's work criticizes the tendency in contemporary church practice to value some forms of work (ministry, teaching, social service) more than others. The hierarchy of the Middle Ages between clergy and laity has now been supplanted by a rift between valued "service professions," which more closely approximate Christian service, and other forms of work such as commerce, industry, and management. Since most Christians do not work in so-called service professions, their work, Larive claims, is considered less intrinsic to faith. The lamentable result is the marginalization of most forms of work to Christian faith. *After Sunday* is one attempt to recover the value and legitimacy of many callings.

Larive recognizes that most work does not offer nests of endless creativity. Most of us, while we work, are not embarking on bold new endeavors, forging novel ideas, or inventing new products. If our work is cocreative, Larive claims, this does not mean that all work is ceaselessly creative. Acknowledging the mundane nature of everyday labor, Larive invokes a Trinitarian framework to discuss the intrinsic value of different kinds of work. The work of the Father/Mother is that which sustains creation, maintaining all that is. Most of the time, Larive claims, our work reflects this dimension of God's work. "Most human work is not new but routine, with a familiar round of sameness. . . . And what is new doesn't spring up out of a vacuum, but, like the increase of knowledge, always rests on the accomplishments of what has gone before."[45] When workers engage in these routines—shopkeeping, answering customers' questions, cleaning, cooking—they engage in acts of maintenance that sustain the world.

Of course, some work does involve the creation of new things: crafting a sculpture, writing a poem, composing a violin concerto, inventing computer software. Larive claims that these forms of work are connected, however tenuously, to the work of the eschatological Christ, the Son who makes all things new. If the work of the Father/Mother is connected to protology, the work of the Son/Christ is related to eschatology. In the midst of all forms of work, furthermore, is the animating power of the Holy Spirit, the Lord and giver of life. The Spirit's work, Larive claims, is connected to the rapport and skill that make good work possible. Holy Spirit both enlivens communities that provide support for workers and bestows the charisma unique to each worker. Larive's point is not to parcel out different branches of work to the distinct persons of the Godhead, as if maintenance were *only* the work of the Father/Mother; rather, his intent is to ground the meaning of humane work in God, and suggest that the diversity of work is precisely what is valued in community and in God. Our cocreativity takes multiple forms as it draws from God's very life.

Miroslav Volf offers a concluding vision of work as cocreative. In *Work in the Spirit*, Volf criticizes the language of vocation for its static rendering of work and human station: God has called me here, and here I will stay. In contrast to what he deems conservative implications of Christian language for vocation and its thin biblical moorings (the Bible uses the language of calling to describe the person's response to God, not his or her occupation), Volf proposes that eschatology and new creation—not call—provide the proper context for understanding human work. "The deepest meaning of human work lies in the cooperation of men and women with God."[46] Volf proposes a thorough restatement of the goodness of creation—creation that is destined for communion with God—and the glimpsing of work within the bounty of creation. Human work matters, as it is given by God in creation, for creation, in anticipation of God's new creation. Just as the "end" for Christians does not stress annihilation, but re-creation and renewal, the end of work is neither disappearance nor apotheosis, but the renewal of work in God's image. Good work, then, anticipates God's transformation of the world.

Each worker plays a distinct and irreplaceable role in the anticipation of

God's reign. Our work is less a calling for Volf than it is a claiming of a particular charisma. His understanding of work is pneumatological, which he claims is more adaptive to the mobility and rapid pace of postindustrial societies. Whereas one seems called to one place, one responds to charisma ever anew in new situations. "All human work, however complicated or simple, is made possible by the operation of the Spirit of God in the working person; and all work whose nature and results reflect the values of the new creation is accomplished under the instruction of the Spirit of God."[47]

These three attempts to reclaim the centrality of creativity in work achieve laudable aims. Each, in their own way, seek to ameliorate the tendency to claim some work (and thus some workers) as more valuable than others. Each, too, aims to integrate core claims of Christian faith with work, so that the activity that occupies most of one's waking hours is not incidental, but fundamental to that faith. The problem, as I see it, with notions of cocreativity is that they may inadvertently emphasize the agency of the creature at the expense of the Creator. None of the works surveyed lapse into this danger, but the risk nonetheless remains. Cocreativity implies a cooperation that is often not present in human labor: most of the time we do not align our work with God's creativity. This danger, perhaps, can be averted by a more realistic—and Reformed—understanding of our work as a response to God's work. Rather than undermining creativity, our responsive labor is always grounded in God's prior activity. Creativity belongs first and foremost to God, who invites us to respond with work of our own, given to others and ultimately back to God. The remainder of this book explores some of the implications of our responsive labors: in Trinitarian theology, in worship, and in the global economy that often denigrates work.

CONCLUSION

Work has received enormously varied attention in the two-thousand-year tradition of Christian theology. At times lamented as curse, at others heralded as a means of fulfillment, work in every age has seemed inescapable, even if the topic has not held the explicit attention of most theologians. In reality, work neither saves nor damns us. The experience of work, for most of us, is more ambiguous: at times reflecting the alienation of humanity from God, at others intimating our communion with the Creator. We are made for work, but not for work alone. Work is doubtless a necessity for human beings, but it is also a gift from the Creator, a gift of self-expression, of community building, and of thanks for the work God has already done. When our work responds to that gift, we catch a glimpse of good work in action.

3

God's Work for Us

Work promises fulfillment in the elusive strains of the American dream: good work provides its own satisfaction while it fuels our consumer habits. We Americans expect much from work, and as a result, we keep working longer hours. As many of us work our fingers to the bone in pursuit of that dream, an increasing number of us struggle to find paid work or work multiple jobs in order to make ends meet. By most measures, we are working a lot. In the midst of this work, we justify both our industrious habits and a necessary level of unemployment. We *must* work hard to maintain a decent standard of living, while others must remain out of work so that incentives for economic growth remain. Work offers its own form of justification, yet it tends to be unsatisfying for many of us. As a society, we are not any more content with our work than we were while we were working less. These attempts to justify ourselves through work also founder when they encounter the gospel, which stresses that we cannot justify ourselves. Before we ever lift a finger in labor, God is already at work, redeeming the world in Jesus Christ. Because this redemption is the grand work of the cosmos, we are freed from the hubris of overestimating our labors and the denigration of believing they are worthless. Good work, as we explore in this chapter, is work that responds to the salvation pulsing at the heart of the universe, revealed in the Triune God of Jesus Christ. That work justifies, fulfills, and shares in abundance, transforming our work as it participates in God's very life. When our work responds to God's gift of Godself, we too can be examples of good work.

The previous chapter surveyed some of the theological attempts to make sense of human labor, attempts that have often hovered on the margins of theological reflection. The turn in this chapter is to place this ever-practical theme closer to the center. But this chapter does not achieve this aim by elevating human work in itself or considering our labors apart from God's grace. A theology of work, properly framed, begins by describing God's work for us: work has meaning, first and foremost, because it is grounded in the life-giving, self-diffusive good of Trinity. The God of Israel and Jesus Christ works for us, freeing us to work for and with each other. As it explores the redemptive work that gives life to the world, this chapter draws on a wealth of resources, revisiting biblical portrayals of God the worker and highlighting some prominent themes in classic Trinitarianism and their recovery by contemporary theology as they describe the self-diffusive goodness of the divine economy. Each of these resources has significantly practical implications for how we construe our own labors as a response to what God has already done in Jesus Christ.

THE CHALLENGE OF GOD-TALK

This attempt to ground anthropology (work is a dimension of anthropology) in the doctrine of God must, however, heed a warning. The danger is that one takes a rough understanding of human work and projects it on God, perhaps with larger and bolder letters. Karl Barth claimed that modern notions of God were often little more than statements about humanity uttered in a loud voice, an indictment that remains relevant today. One danger of a theology of work is that we render God a better and more efficient worker than the latest management gurus have ever dreamed. Clearly, we can commodify God to an idol of our own making, an idol that slips seamlessly into consumer speech. Yet I am also convinced—perhaps more than Barth was—that the only way human beings can talk about God is by drawing on our own language and experience of God. Even when Christians resort to the primary reservoir of Christian language for God, the Bible, we cannot escape the stubborn fact that the God who addresses us in that text is mediated through the human words—and experiences—of the biblical authors and the varied communities that read, edited, and reflected on their words. Experience is essential to Christian theology. Our experiences and language are vehicles for God's address to us, vehicles that speak about God truthfully, albeit partially. Calvin compared Scripture to God's lisp or baby-talk. In order to communicate with us, God condescends to us and accommodates Godself to *our* words, however imperfect, partial, and fragmentary they may be. When we take this recognition seriously, *all* God-talk is provisional, whether found in Scripture, theological classics, or contemporary preaching. Our words convey truth as well as falsehood, beauty as well as ugliness, goodness as well as evil, but the good news is that God can take our words—and work—and address us through them.

One conceivable approach to a theology of work would be to claim that because God works, our human labors become "God-like." I do not follow that course in this chapter. The substance of a theology of work cannot be found in the apotheosis of work: writing, cleaning, teaching, selling, counseling, or managing. God does not divinize our labors in working on our behalf in Jesus Christ. Rather, God desires communion with creatures, a communion that respects rather than obliterates creatureliness. In this communion, we remain ourselves while our labors do not vanish in the divine life. This communion affects every aspect of our lives in the midst of the everyday. God empowers us to respond—in our lives, in our work—to the work God has already done in Jesus Christ. The divine work is that we, too, by grace become participants in the life God gives to creation. Good work is a dim reflection of the life and work of God for the world, a response that enables us by grace to live the communion that is God's very life.

How, then, can we speak about this God of Christian faith? I have already highlighted some challenges of God-talk, whether presented by attributing too much or too little value to our words. Fourth-century theologian Gregory of Nyssa was as aware of these pitfalls as much as writers in these (post)modern times: "We, however, following the suggestions of Holy Scripture, have learned that His nature cannot be named and is ineffable. We say that every name, whether invented by human custom or handed down by the Scriptures, is indicative of our conceptions of the divine nature, but does not signify what that nature is in itself."[1] However much we invoke God's name, the words that form that name will always remain *our* words.

If Christians were to stop with this realization and linger there, silence would be the only appropriate response to God. Silence has a history in Christianity that sustains the life and piety of countless Christians, from early desert hermits to medieval monastics and contemporary Quakers. Yet it is hard to imagine that a faith centered on the Word would insist on silence alone. Despite the inadequacy of our words, Christians have also claimed that we can speak about God because of the economy (God's work) of salvation. God has made Godself known through God's activity on behalf of creation, a work that we experience in our creatureliness. The God who is infinite, ineffable mystery has also spoken in the Word of creation, the Incarnate Word of Jesus Christ, and in the Advocacy of the Holy Spirit. Christians speak about God because God has revealed Godself as a creating, redeeming, and sustaining God in the midst of the everyday. This "facticity of redemption" enables Christians to speak truthfully about God.[2] God reveals Godself as the Redeemer in the work of salvation, the life-giving communion of Father, Son, and Holy Spirit; Creator, Redeemer, Sanctifier; the Mother of us all.

We can speak about God's work, in other words, because God has made

Godself known—in our imperfect words—as the Worker and Bearer of our salvation. In the thirteenth century Thomas Aquinas suggested that our words for God are truthful on the level of analogy:

> Some words are used neither univocally nor purely equivocally of God and creatures, but analogically, for we cannot speak of God at all except in the language we use of creatures, and so whatever is said both of God and creatures is said in virture of the order that creatures have to God as to their source and cause in which all the perfections of things pre-exist transcendentally.[3]

What Thomas means by analogy is not that we transfer our idea of human goodness and render it God's, as if God's goodness were simply the bigger and better version of what we experience as human goodness. Rather, he claims that the primary source of Goodness rests in the Creator, and we experience "goodness" analogically by virtue of the Creator's distribution of goods. Communion, salvation, and work, therefore, are grounded in God's economy. We can speak about God as Worker because God has revealed Godself in Jesus Christ as the One who is at work from the beginning as the Bearer of our salvation. God is the primary worker, and we respond to God's work.

As we remind ourselves of language's provisionality, Christians can speak of God at work for us. God's "first work," creation by the Word, is the release of an other for fellowship and love. God does not create an other by necessity, but by grace, out of delight, pleasure, and goodness. The entire trajectory of salvation history that emerges subsequent to this first work is God's relentless pursuit of maintaining and redeeming fellowship with the Other. God's covenant with Israel, the incarnation of Jesus of Nazareth, the emergence of the Christian church, and the far horizon of Christian hope where God will be "all in all" depict God's irrevocable promise of relationship with God's people. God seeks communion with us, and we are made for communion with God. Sallie McFague has expressed this grand sweep of salvation history rather succinctly: "We (the universe) come from God and return to God, and in the 'interim' we live in the presence of God—even when we do not know or acknowledge it."[4] The God that Christian faith proclaims, even in the inadequacy of our language, is a God who seeks communion, works for communion, and rests in communion with God's creatures.

GOD THE WORKER

The Bible assumes that God works. Creation, covenant, redemption, and consummation do not occur effortlessly by God's inexorable will, but are the result of divine work to maintain relationships. These labors, moreover, are often arduous, invoking the mundane tasks of human life in agrarian societies. The God who fashions a people and assigns them work is also at work in the midst of these tasks, embodying and blessing their very human labors. James Francis notes that "almost every trade and craft is used in the imagery of [biblical] theism e.g. the refiner's fire, the metal worker's forge, irrigation, bleaching, building, pottery, forestry and threshing."[5] As God takes these human labors as God's own, the biblical authors describe a God who is passionately involved with creation and who will work at any cost to preserve the relations that God has labored to establish. God works not out of necessity or compulsion, but in order to share the abundance of God's life with others.

God the Worker directs, acts, and stages the drama of Israel's salvation history, laboring in metaphors close to the hearts and experiences of Israelite workers. The opening scene depicts God as a Gardener who plants the flora and fauna that populate earth: "The LORD God planted a garden in Eden, in the east; and there he put the man whom he had formed" (Gen. 2:8). Agricultural work does not cease with this first act, as God subsequently waters the land (Ps. 104:13), prunes branches to bear fruit (John 15:2), and grafts wild and cultivated olives together to make something new (Rom. 11:24). Renewal of the covenant also hearkens the work of farming. In Nathan's oracle, God "will appoint a place for my people Israel and will plant them, so that they may live in their own place, and be disturbed no more" (2 Sam. 7:10a). Agricultural imagery permeates biblical narratives, depicting God as the source from whom all things grow and bestowing agriculture with a dignity of its own. Labors that sustain the harvest of the land are blessed and claimed by God.

Gardening and farming do not exhaust the metaphors of God's creativity. Skilled trades, such as pottery, often surface in Hebrew Scripture, as when God molds Adam from the moist earth and endows him with the breath of life (Gen. 2:7). Such imagery recurs throughout biblical narratives and appears prominently in the prophecy of Jeremiah. Here, God's creativity bespeaks God's sovereign rule and warns against the pride that would ignore covenant. For Jeremiah, the image of God as potter is meant to comfort as well as jolt: "Can I not do with you, O house of Israel, just as this potter has done? says the LORD. Just like the clay in the potter's hand, so are you in my hand, O house of Israel. At one moment I may declare concerning a nation or a kingdom, that I will pluck up and break down and destroy it" (Jer. 18:6–7). Just as God molds a people as an artful vessel, so too may God break that handiwork and fashion it anew.

As God seeks to maintain and renew covenant with Israel, God's "end work" of judgment and vindication also invokes creative labor such as metalwork and harvesting. Prophetic literature suffuses with such imagery. As precious metal emerges from heat, with dross falling by the wayside, so too God works to ensure the establishment of justice and the purification of God's people. One of the most memorable passages of biblical prophecy captures this strand of work, as it invokes the coming of God's annointed: "But who can endure the day of his coming, and who can stand when he appears? For he is like a refiner's fire and like fullers' soap; he will sit as a refiner and purifier of silver, and he will purify the descendants of Levi and refine them like gold and silver" (Mal. 3:2–3).[6] The image of a metalworker laboring over a forge is prominent in Ezekiel as well, where God's wrath is compared to a smelter: "As one gathers silver, bronze, iron, lead, and tin into a smelter, to blow the fire upon them in order to melt them; so I will gather you in my anger and my wrath, and I will put you in and melt you" (Ezek. 22:20). Though the flames burn hot with anger for Ezekiel's metalworker, the point of this imagery is not the destruction of God's people, but their renewal and reclamation of covenant. Amid the dross emerges a purified remnant that lives in faithfulness to God's promises.

God's end-work of judgment invokes agricultural labors as well. As God plants and waters creation, God reaps, winnows, and threshes when the full harvest appears. In the Gospels, John the Baptist announces the coming Messiah, whose "winnowing fork is in his hand, to clear his threshing floor and to gather the wheat into his granary; but the chaff he will burn with unquenchable fire" (Luke 3:17). Passages such as this reappear throughout the New Testament: the Messiah who announces judgment is also the farmer with a scythe, harvesting abundant grain, separating wheat from chaff (Matt. 9:37–38; 13:30; Mark 4:29; Rev. 14:14–20), endowing the hard work of the harvest with new dignity.

For the Christian imagination, the central thrust of God's work is the incarnation. In the flesh of Jesus of Nazareth, Christians glimpse the intimacy of God's work for creation: in hands that heal, gesture, touch, and are pierced; in arms that embrace, hold, and labor with wood—whether on the carpenter's bench or on the road to Golgotha; in a voice that proclaims the good news and cries out in godforsakenness; in feet that journey from town to town and are nailed to the cross. In Jesus Christ, God's work touches and claims us all. God comes not as the owner of work, not as one with the luxury not to work, but as an ordinary laborer. Jesus Christ dignifies and blesses all human work, and even redeems and transforms the humiliating work that sends him to the cross. Work has meaning because in Jesus Christ God incorporates our labors into the divine life.

From creation to the fulfillment of creation, there is hardly a human craft that does not emerge blessed by God's providential hand. Each moment, each person, each effort of human labor, is sustained by God's work. As Marc Kolden writes, "God is *constantly* creating everything. Nothing exists in itself or on its own. Everything is always being upheld by ongoing divine creative work."[7] Yet the shape of God's work is radically different from the ways in which work is practiced and distributed in ancient societies as well as modern ones. Whereas current patterns of work imply scarcity and competition, the divine work operates out of abundance, generosity, and freedom—seeking to draw all things into deeper communion with God. When God plants, sows, potters, refines, and comes in the flesh of Jesus Christ, gifting marks the divine economy rather than hoarding.[8] God works so that others may have the gift and have it abundantly.

This economy operates with odd assumptions about the nature of work: labor is meant to be shared, work is meant to enrich and sustain the life of creation, work draws us into communion with each other and with God. As the Bible depicts God at work creating, sustaining, refining, and redeeming, nearly every trade of ancient society is invoked. As God is personified in the metalworker, farmer, potter, and forester, we gain greater clarity about the nature of God's work. But something else happens as well: if God can be personified in human trades, might we also suggest that God is also at work redeeming and transforming those very occupations themselves? God's economy of grace, as it takes shape incarnationally, is also operating in the midst of the daily tasks where we find ourselves, transforming them by grace into labors more closely aligned with God's generosity. As God labors on behalf of creation, God also takes our work as God's own. Turning to resources in Trinitarian theology, we see how this economy of grace transforms and redeems our daily, mundane work.

A WORKING DOCTRINE: THE TRINITY AND PRACTICAL THEOLOGY

At this point in the study, it may seem odd to turn toward Christian articulations of the Trinity. Throughout this book, I have strived to stick close to everyday working matters and their intersection with Christian faith. Few doctrines, at least on the surface, seem more remote from the daily toil of workers than the Trinity. Indeed, over the past several centuries—at least since the Middle Ages—the doctrine has become more and more removed from the ordinary piety of Christian life. Even if Christians agree that the Trinity represents one of the fundamental convictions of the faith, most lay and ordained Christians have difficulty relating this doctrine to the practice of faith. In popular imagination, the Trinity connotes the mysterious, inner workings of the Godhead, an abstruse and perhaps dangerous topic best reserved for scholars and theologians. A practical doctrine of the Trinity? At best, this seems an oxymoron.

Even more pernicious is the de facto separation between the Trinity and other claims Christians make about God. By the Middle Ages, the distinction in doctrinal primers between "the One God" and "the Triune God" had become well-fixed. Compendiums of dogma generally treated the classical proofs of God's existence and God's person as Creator under *De Deo Uno*. The doctrine of the Trinity was treated distinctly, as a subject of special revelation, clarifying and enhancing the claims made in discussions of the one God. As a result, the Trinity could seem at times like an appendage to other claims accessible to reason and experience. The "inner life" of God, in this sense, became unhinged from God's work in the economy of redemption, effectively negating patristic insistence that one knows divine life in and through that economy. Karl Rahner has claimed that this separation has accelerated since the Middle Ages. Consider his indictment of modern theology: "Should the doctrine of the Trinity have to be dropped as false, the major part of religious literature could well remain virtually unchanged."[9] Remote from the lives of contemporary Christians, uncoupled from other claims about God that Christians are wont to make, the Trinity in the modern era assumes the false guise as a mystery reserved for specialists.

Nothing could be further from the intent of the doctrine's formulation in the church's early centuries. The emergence of Trinitarian doctrine in that highly charged intersection of Judaic and Hellenistic trajectories was an intensely practical concern. Early exponents of the doctrine were not chiefly concerned with abstruse subjects of God's mystery and person separated from the daily labors of creation; they were not trying to distill the fundamental essence of God. Rather, they were trying to speak the good news of salvation for humankind wrought by God's work in Jesus Christ. The doctrine of the Trinity is about God's gift of salvation in Jesus Christ, our knowledge of salvation from the One God of Israel, and our participation in the new life by the power of the Holy Spirit. These everyday, practical concerns—God's gift of salvation and life lived in response to that gift—lie at the heart of the doctrine's formulation. Catherine LaCugna writes:

> The doctrine of the Trinity is not above all a theory about God's "internal self-relatedness" but an effort to articulate the basic faith of Christians: In Jesus Christ, the ineffable and invisible God saves us from sin and death; by the power of the Holy Spirit, God continues to be altogether present to us, seeking everlasting communion with all creatures.[10]

The Trinity is a statement about God's work of redemption: God's maintenance of the household, creation of new things in the household, and desire to draw all things into full communion in a household of love. The tradition has dubbed this moment the "economic Trinity," God's work in relation to creation that began with the foundation of the cosmos, continues in the gift of covenant, intensifies in the incarnation of Jesus Christ, and accelerates toward the fulfillment of creation when God shall be "all in all." Wherever we are, God is already at work, transforming us and our work into creatures who more nearly reflect God's communion.

The early Christians were convinced that something new was manifested in the life, ministry, death, and resurrection of Jesus Christ—the full presence of God's very self in the flesh. God does not hold back from humanity in the incarnation, but whispers and offers God's fullness. The doctrine of the Trinity, then, did not arise out of speculative concerns about the nature of God's inner person, but out of the practical concern of connecting the salvation proclaimed in Jesus Christ and sustained by the Holy Spirit to the God known in the covenant and people of Israel. Because only God saves, and because early Christians proclaimed salvation in and through Christ, the incarnation was not the creation of another creature, but the gift of God's self for humanity: promised from the foundation of the universe, revealed in the healing, calloused, and crucified hands of a first-century Palestinian Jewish worker. The doctrine began as an expression about the economy—God's work—of salvation. Jesus Christ shows humanity God's work for us in the Spirit, and invites us to participate in that work, as God draws all things into deeper communion.

In Jesus Christ, we behold the pattern of God's life for the world, a pattern of self-communicating, self-giving, self-diffusing love for the sake of life itself. God communicates and gives God's self to the world so that others may live. God's life, in Jesus Christ, becomes in a very real sense *our life*: so that the divine life is nearer to us than our very breath. We live because God lives for us; the Trinity expresses, in doctrine, the shape of God's life for the world. Because we live from that life, it is hard to imagine more practical work.

The next several sections of this chapter examine some implications of Trinitarian theology: how do the claims Christians make about the God at work in creation point to the transformation and redemption of our labors? As I survey themes from writers as varied as fourth-century Cappadocians and twenty-first-century Americans, I connect them to the workers' dilemmas encountered in the first chapter and demonstrate the practical significance of this fundamental Christian doctrine. God's self-disclosure in the economy of salvation points to the intrinsic value of difference, abundance, interdependence, sharing, and play in work. In our economy often characterized by scarcity, a drive toward uniformity, hoarding, poverty, and overwork, God's work reclaims the dignity of our labors. As Christians profess faith in the triune God, they also hope for the transformation of alienated human work as it is enfolded in God's very life.

GOD'S WORK AS AN EMBRACE OF DIFFERENCE

By creating the world, God wills another to be. Trinitarian theology expresses the conviction that who we are and all that we are comes from God. Though God is perfect in Godself, God seeks communion with what is other than God, to share in God's goodness. Trinitarian doctrine teaches that otherness and difference are intrinsic to God's life: both as God creates and releases an Other to be, and as the economy of salvation reveals God to be a communion of divine Persons, engaged in ongoing creative love for the sake of creation. The Father's gift to the world, communicated in the Son and shared in the sanctifying grace of the Holy Spirit, is a gift that seeks an Other.[11]

As God works for the world, sharing Godself with others, that work takes the shape of the divine persons. Meeks writes, "Each person of the Trinity engages in *distinctive personal work*. . . . Each makes a specific contribution to the divine economic work in and for the world." Classical tradition has employed multiple analogies and ways of expressing the distinctive work of each divine Person: the Father's creation, the Son's redemption, and the Spirit's creation anew; the work of loving, being loved, and the expression of love between the two; sending, being sent, and "empowerment of the mission of the Father and the Son."[12] The point of these distinctions is not to parse the divine activity finely, so that the work of the Creator is a discrete endeavor apart from the work of the Redeemer. The point is to recognize that distinctive work is honored and sustained in God's very life as these multiple forms of work are inextricably bound to each other. The work of creating, redeeming, and transforming the world is not a one-time fiat of a divine monarch or the result of three separate decrees, but a movement of distinctive personal work sustained by a community of love. God's work of salvation thrives on difference.

One might suppose that these theological cues would translate seamlessly into rigid divisions of labor, both in the divine economy and the world's. If so, the doctrine of the Trinity would prove a powerfully conservative force: limiting persons to labor in their station, as different labors are assigned to the distinct divine persons and persons created in the divine image. Yet these distinctions in God's life given for the world prove more fluid than fixed. Biblical narratives, for example, speak of God's *ruach* and the Word at work in the creation of the world (Gen. 1:1–2; John 1:1–4); sometimes Jesus sends the Spirit, at other times he is sent by the Spirit (compare John 20:22 and Mark 1:12).[13] These images point, according to John Calvin, not to a "division" but a "real distinction" in the divine economy.[14] Distinction and difference are intrinsic to the divine life, but not in a way that assigns specific tasks only to one person. As we shall explore shortly, these varied works are shared.

Though distinctive work is part of Trinitarian theology, distinctions do not entail the elevating of one form of work over another. Calvin expresses the distinctions as they are interrelated: to the Father is attributed "the beginning of activity, and the fountain and wellspring of all things; to the Son, wisdom, counsel, and the ordered disposition of all things; but to the Spirit is assigned the power and efficacy of that activity." In this relationship, no work is primary while others are secondary. Indeed, Calvin suggests that we should not seek in God's work "a *before* or an *after*,"[15] because the work and relationships of the Trinity are eternal. The activities that form the economy of salvation, therefore, are distinct yet mutually dependent.

As God expresses Godself to creation, God embraces the difference of creation and the difference inherent to the divine life. In sending the Redeemer and aspiring the Sanctifier, the Creator honors the work of each and recognizes that without each person's work, God's self-expression is incomplete. If this is the shape of life given for the world, then it has consequences for our work as well. At a most basic level, Trinitarian doctrine suggests that each person, regardless of age, ability, or status, has distinctive work to bring to the world. As God communicates Godself to us, God blesses creation with difference, and summons us to bring ourselves and our work as a response to that blessing.

This theological insight rings more than a platitude that each person is different, endowed with unique gifts and talents. Indeed, it suggests that to ignore one's gifts (refusing to heed a call to public service, for example) or to misuse them (using one's talents for engineering to design nuclear weapons) is to spurn God's gift of life for the world. Each gift, each work, is irreplaceable as it brings something new to the life of the world. Contrary to patterns of work that see workers as interchangeable cogs, this recognition underscores the infinite value of each worker and the uniqueness of each gift. Second, this affirmation runs counter to patterns of employment in the United States and other developed countries that claim a modicum of unemployment as economically desirable. In response to such systems, Christian theology glimpses waste: when societies assume that not all who want work will find work, they are wasting the gifts God has given. Trinitarian theology, in other words, lends momentum toward the vision of full employment.[16] If God bestows an abundance of different gifts, and relates God's very self to the world in the distinctive work of Father, Son, and Holy Spirit, then this abundance is to be employed in creation to its fullest: when those who seek paid work are without it, the diverse gifts of creation are not adequately employed. In Trinitarian grammar, there is no such thing as an acceptable level of unemployment. God seeks to share Godself with all, and invites us to participate in a communion where there is always enough work to go around.

On the other hand, this theological conviction refuses to reduce human persons to their paid occupations. Not only the gainfully employed make contributions to the common good, but each person, regardless of whether or not they are working. The original giftedness of each person expresses itself with or without a job.[17] Economic productivity or job status is not the chief marker of identity, as much as socialist and capitalist economies suggest otherwise; God, rather, bestows personhood with a gift of grace, a gift that expresses itself to the world uniquely in each person. God's labor in the divine economy suggests that each person is infinitely valuable in its distinctive work. As God gives Godself to the world, we are called to embrace the distinctive contributions of each human person to the common good, work toward a distribution of labor that draws on the richness of all persons, while recognizing that no person is synonymous with his or her work.[18]

INTERDEPENDENT WORK: THE RELATION OF RELATIONS

Trinitarian doctrine ascribes distinction and difference to God's work for the world, rooted in the dynamism that constitutes God's very life. It also highlights the primacy of relationship, grounded in God's self-diffusive love for the world. Gregory of Nyssa, Gregory of Nazianzus, and Basil of Caesarea insisted that the persons of the Trinity had no enduring status apart from each other. One cannot speak of the Son without at the same time invoking the Son's relationship to Father and Spirit. Whatever divine work we address, that work is always dependent on the work of the other two Persons. These relationships, moreover, bear fruit in current understandings of work that stress competition and hierarchy at the expense of relationship and interdependence.

In the late fourth century, Gregory of Nazianzus preached a series of sermons, which have subsequently been dubbed his "Theological Orations." They, along with the writings of his colleagues Gregory of Nyssa and Basil, form a watershed in the formulation of Trinitarian orthodoxy. In one of his orations, Gregory insists that the name Father is "not a name either of an essence or of an action . . . But it is the name of the relation in which the Father stands to the Son, and the Son to the Father."[19] Gregory's understanding of personhood is difficult for moderns to grasp; we are accustomed to thinking of persons as distinct centers of consciousness, marked chiefly by individuality. For Gregory, however, *relationship* is the chief marker of personhood. The divine names signify the endurance of relationships that constitute the life God gives to the world. For Gregory, the beginning of all things and persons is relationship: a relationship to God grounded in God's eternal self-relatedness.

As a fellowship of love, the divine persons work interdependently. Gregory of Nyssa clarifies this point:

> We do not learn that the Father does something on his own, in which the Son does not co-operate. Or again, that the Son acts on his own without the Spirit. Rather does every operation which extends from God to creation and is designated according to our differing conceptions of it have its origin in the Father, proceed through the Son, and reach its completion by the Holy Spirit. . . . Whatever occurs, whether in reference to God's providence for us or to the government and constitution of the universe, occurs through the three Persons, and is not three separate things.[20]

In this cooperation we glimpse unified and purposeful work. Because the work of each person is distinct and interrelated, no person owns, controls, or exploits the work of another. The Cappadocians, perhaps more than their compatriots in the West, ascribed the origin of divine activity in the Father, yet this origination did not result in valuing the Father's work over others', or separating the Father from the other persons. What begins in the Father never remains the Father's alone, but proceeds and aspires through Son and Spirit.[21] In the strictest sense, there is no such thing as the work of the Father apart from the activity of Christ and the Spirit. Classical tradition has dubbed this cooperation of divine work *perichoresis*, the coinherence of each divine Person in the others. God enacts and embodies a genuinely "communal or social work."[22] Whereas we tend to think that cooperation in human labor is necessary because of the inadequacy of individual labors (cooperation mends the lack that each one of us represents), God's *perichoresis* arises not out of imperfection or lack, but out of God's fullness. God's work is cooperative as it expresses the abundance of God's grace for the life of the world. God's benevolent work is not the paternalism that bestows grace on some out of a finite reservoir, so that some may have more and others less; rather, God gives perichoretically out of fullness so that all might live more fully.

Although the Cappadocians claim the Father as the origin of divine work, they also insist on the eternity of divine interdependence. To claim otherwise would be to invoke Arianism or the creatureliness of the Son. Again, Gregory of Nazianzus: "There never was a time when he was without the Word, or when he was not the Father."[23] Isolation in work is foreign to the triune God. Given the modern penchant for determining what belongs to oneself, one's work and one's nation, these strains of divine cooperation have a dissonant ring. As the divine life shakes us free from conceptions of work owned or wielded at others' expense and of personhood embodied apart from others, theology points to a radical revision of work and workers.

To put this revision bluntly, there is no such thing as an individual by herself or himself. As LaCugna puts it, "To be a person is to be defined by where a person comes from; *what a person is in itself or by itself cannot be determined.* The Father comes from no one, the Son is begotten by the Father, the Spirit proceeds from the Father."[24] Such claims arise not out of abstruse speculations about God's nature. Rather, they emerge from the experiences of redemption in Christian community: being founded and claimed by God, redeemed by Jesus Christ, sustained and empowered by the Holy Spirit. For Christian faith, it is nonsensical to talk about one of these experiences apart from the others: every instance of being redeemed by Christ is also rooted in God's originating creative grace and the Spirit's ongoing power. We claim that the work of divine activity is shared because it is experienced and revealed as interdependent work. God does not act as a solitary monarch, but shares abundance with all, expressing God's fullness in interdependent relations, revealed to God's creatures as God draws us closer to the divine light.

As human persons respond to God's creative, redemptive, sustaining work, at least two consequences emerge for how we envision human labors. First, the cooperation of divine activity shows us that fullness is achieved not through competition for scarce resources or the elevation of some workers over others, but in the recognition that one's work is incomplete without the work of others. Indeed, close examination of any kind of work reveals that this is the case. My own field of work—theology—is premised on the enterprise of faith seeking understanding. In seeking a fuller understanding of God's love for the world, theologians constantly fall back on the work of others, contemporaries and ancients who have struggled with the same questions. Theologians read and argue with the work of others, applaud and critique, learning from others' voices as they find their own. Once theologians offer a voice, moreover, they submit their claims to a wider public—church and academy— who may contest, applaud, critique, and even reject their work. Theology is premised on the work of others, and not merely the work of other theologians. Economics, philosophy, literature, and psychology—to name a few disciplines—constantly inform a theologian's work. Much the same could be said of the natural sciences, the arts, law, technology, education, banking, construction, and mercantile trades. There is no such thing as work one does alone; good work always owes itself to other workers.

If interdependence permeates all forms of work, then the attempt to elevate one worker over another is as economically vain as it is theologically misguided. God's economy displays no hierarchy of work other than that between the Creator and creation, and since none of us occupies the space of Creator, hierarchies of work that view some work as "more important" than others are mistaken. The point of this insight is not to create a Maoist utopia, where scholars are forced out of libraries and into rice paddies, but to recognize that the work of the scholar is as dependent upon the farmer as the farmer's is upon the scholar's. It is easy to see how scholars—and other workers—are dependent on farmers: without daily bread, no one can work. But farmers are also dependent on scholars in the sense that the research scholars perform can result in agricultural productivity (technical scholarship), and that scholars explore goodness, truth, and beauty that enrich and dignify the lives of farmers and all workers. The divine economy embraces all work undertaken for the sake of life, and guards against the tendency to think that some forms of work—and, hence, some workers—are worthier than others.

Second, the divine economy underscores the primacy of relation and the priority of persons over labor. Father, Son, and Spirit name relationships that engender good work. What endures in the divine economy are not particular tasks, but the relationships that magnify and share God's life with others. God creates, redeems, and sanctifies because God seeks relation with others. Others are the *point* of God's work. As we respond to the divine work, our labors, too, are designed for others. Good work has value because it enhances and enlivens relationships. The interdependence of work means that every kind of work in the global economy is bound together, for good or for ill. Even in cases where one does not have direct contact with another worker—as is the case between me and the designers and marketers of the word-processing software that allows me to put words on a page—the relationships between workers are mended or broken because of good or bad work. Just as good computer design can enhance writing that gives birth to novels the world enjoys, deleterious work can destroy relationships between creatures, as in check-cashing outfits that gouge the poor and advertising campaigns that denigrate women as sexual objects.

One test of good work is how it enhances or destroys the relationships and people that make life possible. As we respond to God's creative work, the modern tendency to view people as dispensable workers, those who can be dismissed in the name of greater efficiency and market impact, comes into question. Workers always take priority over the work being done. Good work sticks close to the faces and hands of the workers pursuing that aim. In the divine economy, work has a decidedly personal face.

SHARING IN THE DIVINE ECONOMY

The God revealed in the economy of salvation shares God's very self with all creation. As he expressed this theme, Gregory of Nyssa portrays God sharing without remainder in the work of Father, Son, and Holy Spirit. If we inquire after the source of our lives, we cannot discern what comes from the Spirit apart from Christ and the Creator. Rather, Gregory insists, our life is "the same life which is produced by the Father, prepared by the Son, and depends on the will of the Holy Spirit."[25] Notice how Gregory both distinguishes the work of the divine persons and expresses the sharing of a common labor: bestowing others with the gift of life. In this way Gregory preserves distinctions by anchoring personhood in an economy of gift and sharing. The divine persons are what they are only within this eternal relationship and in the sharing of work, not abstracted from that relationship or removed from the economy of redemption. For this reason, Gregory claims, no activity of God can be ascribed to one person alone "as if it were brought to completion individually by each of them or separately apart from their joint supervision. Rather is all providence, care and direction of everything, whether in the sensible creation or of heavenly nature, one and not three."[26] God's work is to share.

In a consumer era, we have become convinced that to share anything—one's possessions, work, food, house, or even oneself—means necessarily that one will have less as a result of sharing. One shares in this context only if one has secured enough for oneself; otherwise, sharing devolves into squandering. How strange, then, resound the echoes of the divine economy, where sharing results not in depletion but greater fullness made possible by divine abundance. The Creator shares with creation not to the diminishment of God's self; God does not have less so that creation can have more. The begetting of the Son does not mean that the Father has less. Rather, God shares so that all might participate in God's fullness. As Kathryn Tanner writes, "What the first Person of the Trinity is essentially is communicated totally or completely to the other two, without the loss or depletion of what the first is and remains."[27] God's giving of self to another means that life abundant is to be shared; in the abundant life, moreover, there is always more than enough work to go around.

Indeed, this triune pattern proves some of the consumer economy's assumptions counterproductive: only when goods and work are hoarded is there less to go around. Our attempts to secure ourselves through possessions or our own work invariably mean that the abundance of creation will not extend to some. What scandal it is when work is hoarded by some so that others may have less. God shares so that all might have more, not that some might have less. Such a claim is not pie-in-the-sky idealism, or an exhortation to share more of ourselves; rather, as God shares out of abundance with creation, giving it life, this pattern is woven into the fabric of the cosmos. Sharing is the true pattern of our life and work. As a pattern of work, moreover, sharing is contagious. For as soon as I share some of myself and my work with another, that other shares anew. Whereas hoarding is finite (one can only hoard so much), sharing is infinite as it gives birth to further acts of sharing. Christians remember the life that sharing makes possible because it is enacted every time we break bread and drink the cup.

This sharing of divine work points to unity in the economy of salvation. All that the Father has is communicated and given to the Son and the Spirit; or, as fourth-century theologian Athanasius puts it, "All things which the Father does and gives he does and supplies through [the Son]."[28] Distinct persons and activity result in a perfect unity of work, so that all might participate in God's fullness. Sharing in the divine economy does not result in a dispersal or fragmentation of purpose, but in an intensification of the divine aim to be all in all. Sharing, in the divine economy, always begets more.

What distinguishes the divine economy from human attempts to ensure sharing—whether by benevolent taxation policies, radical redistributive programs, or attempts at cooperatives—is that God shares without coercion. God neither forces the creature to receive God's grace nor demands that sharing epitomize the life of graced creation. Forced sharing is oxymoronic. Sharing cannot be coerced; otherwise it ceases to be sharing. God's sharing, by contrast, is free; the work of the divine persons lures creation into the fuller life that results from the free gift of God's self to the world. The sharing of God's self with creation is so respectful of personhood, so uncoercive, that God enables creatures to say "no" to that gift. The paradox is that we typically say no. In response to God's sharing, we choose to hoard what we think is ours, and thus choose death.

These reflections on divine sharing, among the Trinitarian persons and between God and creation, have obvious implications for the revision of human work. Recalling the earlier discussion of unemployment, poverty, and the working poor in chapter 1, we can observe how contradictory contemporary working practices are for the life of the commonweal. Much work in contemporary America is hoarded. We accustom ourselves to the view that there is not enough work to go around and that illegal immigrants from Mexico, therefore, are a threat to American workers. Some degree of poverty and unemployment is inevitable and desirable, moreover, for the economy to produce sustainable growth and as a motivation for others to work. One must work if one is to avoid the trap of poverty. I must hang onto my job if I am to secure myself. The results of this hoarding, however, breed disastrous results: immigrants who labor under secrecy, without insurance, while engaged in often dangerous occupations; many others who seek work are unemployed or underemployed. Meanwhile, the ranks of the working poor are swelling, proving the point that work alone is no securer of a living wage. Benefits are being slashed in an era of corporate downsizing, so that health insurance becomes a dispensable luxury provided by corporate planners (who are insured without question). We are living amid the contradictions of pursuing economic growth when work is not shared, which has recently resulted in stagnation.[29]

In contrast, a vision of work that responds to God's fullness recognizes that it is not beneficial to any society to have millions unemployed or underemployed. A society that tolerates unemployment is a society convinced that gifts are not meant to be shared. A society that responded to God's economy would work toward the vision of full employment, recognizing that there is always sufficient work as long as there are people in God's world. Yet full employment does not mean forced policies of workfare or the stipulation that in order to receive government assistance one *must* work. Recent attempts along these lines reflect the human propensity to value some persons more than others: the "deserving" poor, as a matter of course, should have greater access to the goods of society than the "undeserving." This propensity flies in the face of the theology of work developed along Trinitarian lines: a theology that assumes an inestimable value of *each* person, regardless of work; a theology that operates out of assumptions of sharing and abundance instead of hoarding and hierarchy among workers. Instead of workfare, a society that envisioned full employment and the full utilization of persons' gifts would provide opportunities for vocational training, further education, and transportation to work for those who need it.[30] For example, if a society needs more computer technicians, and if such positions redound to greater quality of life shared among many, then a society should establish the means to train the requisite technicians. Once all other options were exhausted for particular workers, the government could become the employer of last resort, offering short-term work in areas where civic need is highest. Such policies would not distinguish between "worthy" and "unworthy" citizens, but offer means of fuller participation in society and in the abundance of workers' gifts. Forced work is not shared work. The shared work that we are given is a gift and a response to grace, not a demand.[31]

THE PLAYFULNESS OF DIVINE WORK

The distinction between force and freedom helps us distinguish between alienated labor and self-expression in work while it also recalls a key component of divine work that has rarely captured the attention of theology: playfulness. This absence is surprising, given the prominence of delight and pleasure that pervades biblical narratives. In Scripture God does not work compulsively, begrudgingly, or acquisitively—oft-cited markers of a consumer economy—but out of the delight of sharing God's self with another. Though God labors continuously on our behalf, this labor is an expression of good pleasure.

In the supposed stodginess of nineteenth-century German academe, G. W. F. Hegel emphasized the playfulness of God's work anchored in the Trinitarian life. For Hegel, God is the Absolute Subject who seeks an Other, to give Godself to another. This drive means that self-differentiation is intrinsic to God's being: self-differentiation is the way God communicates Godself to the world, grounded in the eternal self-communication of the Trinity. This "act of differentiation," Hegel claims, is "a play of love with itself."[32] God's love is self-communicative and playful, never imposing itself upon another, but gifting another with life. The eternal begetting of the Son by the Father is echoed in God's creation of the world: both, as the expression of self-communicative love, entail the release of another to be in freedom.[33] God's work for creation is never coercive, but a playful release of love that allows the world to be. God's delight is the creation of free creatures who respond to the Creator, not dictating that creatures respond to God in a certain way. The Trinity, for Hegel, thus symbolizes the eternal play of God's good work, work that spills out into a world of freedom.

God's play at work, however, does not mean the divine economy is a stranger to the rupture, tragedy, scorn, and alienation of labor. God's delight does not ignore the ways in which labor and relationships are broken continually in creation. Indeed, as the incarnation and cross remind us, God plunges headlong into those chasms. For this reason, Hegel warned that the idea of the play of love with itself "sinks into the realm of what is merely edifying, and even insipid, if the seriousness, the anguish, the patience, and the labor of the negative are lacking from it."[34] God's play, in other words, is not a diversion from work, but a component of God's purposeful work of establishing communion with creation. The overarching theme of this work is delight: the free expression of God's goodness and love shared with the creature. But in seeking this aim, pursuing this work, God also opens Godself to the scorn, rejection, and alienation of the creature. God's work of extending delight and play to creation also means that the Redeemer faces the cross. In rejecting God's work, anguish results. Play, in other words, is not an end in itself or an escape from work, but the result of God's radical work of love for creation.

A humane vision of our work requires an element of play, not as diversion, but as a reminder that work is an expression of self as much as it is a means to a living. For too many, work has lost its potential as a means of self-expression as we respond to God's gift and becomes drudgery and toil: thank God it's Friday. If recent job satisfaction surveys are accurate, countless workers feel dominated by their work. But if play is a characteristic of divine work, we might respond to the Creator's delight in us by recovering play in our own work.

What would play at work resemble? First, playful work would allow workers to find satisfaction, and at times even delight in the fruits of their labors.

One means of achieving this would be to broaden programs of worker participation in management decisions. Such policies would intensify the participation of all employees in the collective work of a firm. If one obstacle to play and self-expression is the sense that one's work is owned by another person, policies that expand shared ownership might contribute toward mutual delight in work where all workers have a voice.

Yet such programs cannot be justified on the basis of productivity alone. Work in the divine economy also reveals that production is not an ultimate value. What endures are the relationships made possible through God's work: both the eternal relation of the divine persons and God's promise of eternal life to the creature with the Creator. Human work that responds to this kind of work will offer occasions, space, and time for the development of self-expression with others through work. God's labor shows that work is not drudgery, but enables us to develop relationships with others so that all might live more abundantly. To lose oneself in playful work is not the aim; rather, one point of playful work is to deepen communion with others as one expresses oneself in work, delighting in the divine work that sustains the world.

Such accounts of play, however, risk blurring the distinction between work and play. If good work contains an element of play, it also entails time away from the job. Leisure has become a scarce commodity in our overworked society. It is now normal to skimp on time off and check e-mail on the few occasions that we have a vacation. God's work disrupts this pattern of normalcy, reminding us that work is not the end of human being. We are, in life and death, in rest and work, to "glorify God and to enjoy him forever."[35] Glorifying and enjoying communion with God, however, does not stem from our work; God, rather, gives us God's self unreservedly and without remainder. We cannot work ourselves into relationship with God; we must, instead, rest in that relation. In an overworked society, this knowledge rings as good news. Yet we usually ignore its chorus. Believing we can work our way to happiness, we are engulfed in frenzies so that even while away from the job, we continue to think about work. The glut of e-mail, the gradual eclipse of down time by on-the-job demands, and the reality of moonlighting in order to make a living wage have all contributed to an atmosphere where leisure is preciously scarce.

A society that values workers and the work they produce would insist on vacation time for *all* workers. American law does not mandate a week of paid leave, and thus betrays our regard of workers as inexhaustible commodities. The cycle of God's activity, as narrated in Genesis 1, points to a different pattern: on the seventh day God rests. God does not rest because God's work is finished; God rests in order to set in motion the cosmic balance that sustains life. Work alone may provide initial fruit, but it will soon degenerate into ceaseless toil, the depletion of the soil, and the degradation of the human person. Israel's Sabbath laws codify that people do not live from work, but from God's life. Good work, so it seems, is bound up with ample rest.

Situating rest within the span of work, moreover, guards against the tendency in consumer societies to see leisure time as the reward of hard work. Americans are particularly baffling in this pursuit. A casual glance at any supermarket magazine rack reveals glossy-paged endorsements of high-octane leisure activities that Americans attack with manic speed. For those who can afford it, no vacation is exotic enough, no activity "extreme" enough. The proliferation of Everest expeditions (often by rather novice climbers), extreme sports, eco-tourism on distant continents, and insanely packed holidays (eight countries in seven days!) all confirm the American tendency to equate more with better. A bumper-sticker popular in the 1980s also captures this frenzied mood: "He who dies with the most toys wins." Such patterns assume that leisure can only be enjoyed at the end of hard work: Put in enough hours at the office, factory, construction site, and you too can have a dream vacation. But this maddening pursuit of leisure soon proves empty: working hard at thrill-seeking exhausts body and spirit as it deadens our sense of thrill; manic holidays leave little time for rest; ravenous appetites for toys are never satisfied. Leisure, in other words, cannot be peddled as a commodity or held as a carrot at the end of a stick. Instead, as the pattern of God's work for the cosmos shows, good rest comes in the midst of good work, where time is set aside, away from work, for no purposeful activity other than to rest and enjoy the world, one's companions, and the God who makes all things new. Such rest is a component of good work, but more importantly, frees us from false dependence on our own work. We can rest and say that we have worked enough, in the end, because God is already at work for us.

TRIUNE WORK AND OUR WORK

Human work has meaning because our work is claimed, blessed, and redeemed by God. As the triune God transforms our work, we are made participants in God's life. Because God is at work in us, statements about the Trinity are also statements about our own lives. Karl Rahner lamented the gradual separation of God's "inner life" from the life of humanity as a theological disaster. The tendency to abstract the immanent Trinity from the economy of salvation was, in the end, a failure to speak the good news: "The isolation of the treatise of the Trinity *has* to be wrong. There *must* be a connection between Trinity and man. The Trinity is a mystery of *salvation*, otherwise it would never have been revealed."[36] Rahner's point is enormously practical: as we are redeemed by God, the triune work gradually gives shape to our own work.

In the early church, Athanasius stressed this practical importance of Trinitarian faith. Jesus Christ, fully human and fully divine, brings human work to God while he also represents God's work for us. What happens in Jesus happens to *all* humanity: "When the Lord, as a man, was washed in the Jordan, we were the ones washed in him and by him. And when he received the Spirit, we were the ones who became recipients of the Spirit through him."[37] In Jesus Christ, God's life becomes the life of the world. To understand humane work, we look first to God. Catherine LaCugna makes this point emphatically: "The life of God is not something that belongs to God alone. *Trinitarian life is also our life*. . . . Followers of Christ are made sharers in the very life of God, partakers of divinity as they are transformed and perfected by the Spirit of God."[38] God extends grace to us, that we might enjoy communion with God and one another forever. As God redeems our lives, nothing in our lives is discarded, forgotten, or erased. The incarnation of the Redeemer includes his hand-work as carpenter and healer, his teaching, his preaching, and his bearing of the cross: work of God that becomes our work as well. Because the Redeemer experienced suffering and became sin for our sake means that redeemed life and work encompasses our suffering. Though consummated life includes the promise of every tear wiped from our eyes, each of our tears is preserved in God's life.

We live in this "in between" time: after the appearance of the Redeemer but before the final tear will be wiped from our eyes. God's work is already redeeming our work, but that work is not yet redeemed fully. In the meantime we work, at times in ways that reflect—however dimly—the grace of the Creator, at others in defiance of grace and in alienation from one another. How does the world receive this graceful work of the Creator? We cannot say that the world bears no imprint of God's work on its behalf. If we claim as much, then God is not a self-communicating God, and the doctrine of Trinity has no grounding in the economy of redemption. The world *does* receive the communication of God's very self, but incompletely and imperfectly. We receive God's work partially, on the way to full communion with God. As Kathryn Tanner writes, "The world as it comes to be and takes shape from God reflects the dynamics of the trinitarian life. The world does so, however, in a nondivine and therefore only approximate fashion."[39] We come from God, live from God, and in the midst of all that alienates and separates humanity from one another and from God, we are on our way to God because of God's work. That work gives us hope for our own.

In a society where job satisfaction has proven elusive, this description of God's work for us should give us pause. Part of our dilemma is that we seek satisfaction in transitory things that cannot satisfy: the right job, the right friends, the right things. One practical consequence of Trinitarian faith is in the straightforward claim that our work alone and things alone cannot satisfy the human creature. Once we place the quest for satisfaction in something that we do, the factory of idols spins its maddening wheels. We then seek satisfaction in something that we create, something that will always prove empty, no matter how hard we work at it. The chief end of the creature is communion with God, work that God alone provides for us. God's work and life satisfy the creature—a recognition that should give us at least a moment of rest.

While we rest in God, however, fulfilling work is yet possible. The key lies in viewing our work as a *response*—however imperfect, however faulty—to the work that God has already accomplished for us. Any work that human beings do—so long as it is for the sake of life—can be glimpsed as a response to God's creative, sustaining, and life-giving work. Work that fulfills need not only be found in the so-called service professions such as medicine, counseling, and social work, where the response to God's work may seem most obvious. Rather, work that fulfills is any work that seeks to express oneself for another: building a house, selling clothes stitched with care, investing money responsibly with an eye to the common good, policing streets so that all might thrive in the city. Any work that we are given for the sake of community can be a response to the work God has already done. Such work is satisfying not because it is the sole source of the worker's satisfaction and identity, but because it is grounded in God's work on behalf of the world. As we yearn for God, that kind of work satisfies the hungry heart.

THE RELATIVE VALUE OF HUMAN WORK

As God labors for us, our work is eternally valued and relativized in the triune life. Both of these components—value and the surrender of value—are essential for a theology of work. On the one hand, as God takes our work as God's own in Jesus Christ, human work has eternal value. What we do with the time we have *matters*. It matters that we make use of the gifts God has given us; it matters that we work toward the vision of the peaceable reign, just as it mattered that Jesus worked with his hands, touching and blessing children and lepers. As the Word takes flesh in the calloused hands of a carpenter, God values *all* human trades in their particularity. Jesus engaged in particular work and directed his work toward the coming of God's reign, thereby granting blessing and meaning to our unique work. When Christians value human work, they also anticipate the hope of work's transformation, where God will be all in all. Christian faith, in the mainstream, has never embraced annihilationism, the idea that God will destroy the present order, erase all within it, and begin creation de novo. Christians reject annihilation because in Christ God is already at work renewing and re-creating the present order, a renewal that suffuses all things.[40] The products of our labors and the energy of our work, Christian faith claims, will be renewed in the New Jerusalem. The life of the new creation, in the vivid account of John's apocalypse, is not characterized by endless lollygagging in celestial bliss, but by the energy of a city: a city that is the product of human hands, renewed by God's providential work. This transformation of human work means that some aspect of our work—however difficult that is to imagine—will have abiding significance in the consummation of creation. The work we do matters.

At the same time, however, this valuing of human work does not result in an overestimation of work as if it were the end of human being. Christian eschatology points to one work at the center of creation: God's economy of blessing, saving, and renewing creation. Because God is already at work renewing creation, our work is relativized. As Meeks writes, "God's gracious justification means that no one must justify himself or herself through work nor does anyone have to create or realize himself or herself through work."[41] The wisdom of Reformation teaching in an age that hoards work is this: work does not set us free. We are justified by grace through faith, not because of the work we do. The measure of our personhood is not the labor we undertake, however lofty or mundane. Rather, our measure is that God has already adopted us as children. We are not what we do; we are whose we are. Modern ideologies dupe us by claiming that we free and create ourselves through our labors or that our work is the measure of our worthiness. Only the Truth will set us free (John 8:32), the truth that we belong to God. God's grace, in Jesus Christ, is true freedom, setting us free to pursue whatever work we do with joy and thanks, humility and attention, instead of attachment, boredom, and dread. As God's grace sets us free, our work has relative value as it becomes aligned with God's extension of communion to all.[42] In response to that work, we worship and give thanks, glorifying the One who sets us free. God's work gives rise to our worship in thanks and praise, rhythms that further specify the shape of our own good work.

4

Work of the People

Liturgy, Eucharist, and Gestures of Good Work

Human persons worship. Expressions of praise and thanks endure across time, culture, and locale. The activities that constitute worship across cultures are the product of our work: oblations, prayers, offerings, music, and lamentations are all the results of hands, heads, hearts, and lungs. Worship is our work at the same time that it belongs to God. Like all other human endeavors, this work can be twisted to idolatrous and destructive purposes. When we render our work to God, however, worship reorients us to God's work, drawing us as participants in the transformation of the world.

Though all aspects of Christian worship—prayer, preaching, meditation on the Word, confession, and offering—anticipate this transformation, in this chapter I focus on a specific practice in worship: the Lord's Supper. This focus on the Eucharist is not meant to the exclusion of other, equally important focal points of Christian worship, such as prayer, preaching, and offering. Celebration of the Eucharist always occurs within a wider scope of Christian practices whenever two or three are gathered in Christ's name. The Eucharist alone, in other words, is neither the sum of Christian worship nor the sole antidote to a revitalization of human work. But the Eucharist does capture the dynamics of God's giving and work that we have already examined, and its celebration draws us into those rhythms, perhaps more vividly than any other Christian practice. For these reasons and in the interest of space, the chapter offers a eucharistic reading of work. It turns first to matters of definition, then considers how the Eucharist challenges our understandings of basic themes in human work: place, time, things, and gift. Amid the holy things of eucharistic celebration lie resources for recovering the holy in the mundane. Second, the chapter considers how the practice of Holy Communion anticipates the transformation of the

67

world already accomplished in Jesus Christ. I then conclude with a brief meditation on four eucharistic gestures—taking, blessing, breaking, and giving—
and how they contribute to a vision of redeemed work. Throughout the chapter
I employ eclectic resources—from patristic writings to contemporary Protestant, Roman Catholic, and Eastern Orthodox theologians. Despite these ecumenical resonances, the reader will detect a Reformed sensibility on most
pages. Across these traditions, commonalities emerge, one of which is the conviction that eucharistic theology is preeminently practical, as celebrating the
Lord's Supper changes us and our work.

PRELIMINARY DEFINITIONS

Countless volumes delineate the contours of the terms that occupy most of
this chapter: worship, liturgy, sacrament, Eucharist. For the purposes of this
study, however, "worship" is the most general term. Any way that human persons seek to glorify God can constitute worship. In this view, worship occurs
on Sundays at cathedrals, house meetings, and camp revivals, in ritualized
action of God's people at specific times and places. But, if the chief end of
humanity, according to the Westminster Confession, is "to glorify God, and
to enjoy him forever," then it impoverishes our view of worship if we restrict
it only to ritual actions performed on Sunday mornings. For this reason, I
would argue that worship also occurs outside particular assemblies: whenever
we glorify God we are worshiping. Spontaneous outbursts of thanksgiving on
backpacking trips are acts of worship. So, too, can be the ways we interact with
coworkers. When I am conscious of the image of God that embraces a
coworker, when I consider her a gift from God and we pursue common work
together, that may be a small act of praise and worship. The current Constitution of the Presbyterian Church (U.S.A.) also echoes this sentiment: "God
hallows daily life, and daily life provides opportunity for holy living. As Christians honor and serve God in daily life, they worship God. For Christians,
work and worship cannot be separated."[1] Clearly, distinctions between work
and worship remain, chief of which is that work is not the end of human
beings. But worship informs and shapes good work, as we give praise in the
midst of work to the God who works on our behalf.

If worship is the more general term for glorifying God, liturgy is more
focused: the distinctive pattern and *ordo* of Christian worship. Liturgy comprises the practices handed down throughout generations of the Christian
church. Justin Martyr, writing in the second century, notes the most enduring
of them: assembly, reading of Scripture, preaching, prayers, thanksgiving over
food, eating and drinking, and a collection for the poor.[2] The repeated actions

of liturgy mold us, inculcating God's gift to us, modeling our response to the gift that claims us. In the rhythm of Christian liturgy, we respond to God in thanksgiving and become more fully who we are, creatures made for God's blessing who live from blessing.

The word "liturgy" owes its origin to two Greek words, *ergon* (work) and *laos* (people). According to this etymology, the practices of Christian worship are not rituals performed by specialists (priests, ministers, deacons) for consumption by the uninitiated; worship, rather, represents the "work of the people." One of the tragedies in the history of the Christian church is that assemblies often forget this: from medieval practices that considered priests and sacraments dispensaries of divine grace, to contemporary mega-churches that foster lay passivity as actors on stage purvey worship as entertainment, mimicking television. Worship is not a commodity, but involves us, body and soul. As Alexander Schmemann writes, the original meaning of *leitourgia* is "an action by which a group of people become something corporately which they had not been as a mere collection of individuals—a whole greater than the sum of its parts."[3] We become, in worship, who we are, in no small part because of others' work. In and through each other's work, we are summoned into the presence of the holy, where we behold God's work.

Reformed traditions have insisted generally that we worship in order to glorify God. Though there are many purposes to worship—to comfort the afflicted, to denounce injustice and announce the reign of God—each of these purposes seeks to give God the glory. The work of corporate worship does not propitiate God or count as a good work, but is a response to grace already given. As it stresses thanksgiving for God's blessing, confession of sin, the encounter with the Word in Scripture and sacrament, and the response to that Word in preaching, offering, and prayer, Reformed worship has a dialogical character: "We hear of God's graceful saving goodness and respond in gratitude, *charis* and *eucharistia*."[4] The basic movements of Reformed worship, à la Calvin, reflect God's address to us and our response to that Word: "No meeting of the church should take place without the Word, prayers, partaking of the Supper, and almsgiving."[5] God's work and our work are intertwined in Christian liturgy, though God's word and work always initiate our own.

Though subsequent Reformed Christians often ignored Calvin's lead, Reformed liturgy initiates the congregation to a sacramental universe, as no meeting takes place without the Lord's Supper. For Calvin, the sacraments were indispensable for God's address to humankind. A sacrament is "an outward sign by which the Lord seals on our consciences the promises of his good will toward us in order to sustain the weakness of our faith."[6] The infinite mystery of God's Word seeks tangible, fleshy form in human words and things of creation. Central to Calvin's view of Word and sacrament is his notion of accommodation: God accommodates Godself to Scripture, bread, and wine so that we can hear, taste, and see that the Lord is good. Just as Scripture constitutes God's "lisp" to us (the accommodation of the divine Word to human words), God shows us the mystery of Christ's union with us "in visible signs best adapted to our small capacity." The bread and wine of the Supper "represent for us the invisible food that we receive from the flesh and blood of Christ."[7] The sacraments, for Calvin as Augustine, are "visible words," by which God expresses the promises of grace and communion in and through Jesus Christ. As we hunger and thirst, those words invite us to drink and never thirst again, eat and never hunger again, and share food and drink with all who hunger and thirst.[8] Word and sacrament, in other words, cannot be severed from each other.

As I noted in the understanding of liturgy more generally, the sacraments might also be described as "an audible and visible *conversation*."[9] God promises us grace and life eternal; we, in turn, bring to the celebration of those promises bread baked with human hands and wine pressed with human feet; we offer these gifts again to God, and God responds by giving God's very self through them, again and again. This conversation, which God always initiates, where God is always taking our work as God's own, is part of what happens whenever the church celebrates Holy Communion. If worship expresses the work of the people, that work always tethers us to God's claim on our whole lives, a claim that gives us rest.

LITURGICAL WORK AND REST

Christian worship, which represents the work of the people, also sets limits to human work. As Sunday worship recalls the Jewish practice of Sabbath, this holy day reminds us that work is not the end of human be-ing. However much the disappearance of blue laws suggests otherwise, however much e-mail claims our "urgent" attention, on the Lord's Day, God calls us to rest. Miroslav Volf has claimed that the "central leisure activity in a Christian concept of the good life [is] communion with God." Cultivation of this good life requires a "need for a special time of communion with God." The rhythms of Christian worship, in part, supply that need. In the assembly of believers, all human work is relativized. What endures for the sake of Christian communion is not one's work as a plumber, accountant, or coach, but God's work on our behalf. In worship, we can pause from labor that exhausts and stultifies, or exaggerates our selfhood, and "anticipate the enjoyment of God in the new creation where [we] will continually dwell with the triune God and the triune God will dwell with us."[10] Because God is already at work, establishing and reestablishing communion, we can rest. Communion frames a proper understanding of the place of work in life: work is for the sake of communion, not communion for the sake of work.

Authentic worship marks the patterns of leisure, work, and the good life: work, rest, taste, and see that the Lord is good. Yet this correlation of leisure and worship runs a risk in a consumer society accustomed to equating rest with entertainment. If we understand worship only as an expression of leisure, worship can become a spectator endeavor, or worse yet, a commodity peddled on the open market. In an era of church shopping, where persons attend the church that fits most with their needs, providing the liveliest music and most engaging preaching, we can construe worship as a restful endeavor that summons little of our effort. Though worship sets appropriate limits to work, it should not release us from work; when we cease working, when we worship only as a spectator, when we see the church as a dispensary of grace offering holy tidbits we consume, we are no longer engaging in the work of the people.

Persons, after all, are the ones who worship. Though Christians celebrate God's work of creation, redemption, and consummation Sunday after Sunday, worship is also an expression of *our* work. The basic patterns of worship that cut across denominations—assembling, proclaiming, offering, singing, praying, giving, confessing—are all expressions of the diverse work that human beings do. None is exhaustive in itself; together all seek to give voice to the work behind all workers: God's desire for communion with all in Jesus Christ. Yet the basic activities of worship are not God's activities: God's voice does not boom from the pulpit, God's prayers do not resound in the sanctuary, however much God takes preaching and prayer as God's own. If we equate our work, voice, or prayer with God's we become idolaters. A Reformed understanding of worship always makes a clear distinction between the work of the people and God's work, knowing that the former is celebrated as holy insofar as it points to the latter. This is the "Protestant principle" that lurks behind Reformed liturgies, which refuses to reduce the transcendent to the work of our hands and voices.[11] Nonetheless, the Reformed heritage also affirms that God works through our hands and voices: God takes our words and gestures and speaks to God's people with them. When the sacraments are rightly administered, there the people encounter God's Word; when Scripture is faithfully proclaimed, God addresses God's people truthfully. Our work and words are not sham efforts, but reflect God's work on behalf of us.

God addresses the Christian assembly through *imperfect* and *flawed* work. Liturgy does not offer model work insofar as it is unblemished by human error and self-interest. Rather, God addresses humanity in the banal, humorous, and even shoddy work of human hands and hearts. God's Word does not require a professional choir, eloquent prayers, choicely tailored liturgical garb, or record-breaking offerings (though none of these should be disparaged for the work they represent). Hymns sung off-key, words stuttered over Communion elements, a simple robe, and an offering that gives something of oneself will do. God takes our work in liturgy—however lofty or humble—blesses them, and takes them as faithful, even truthful, expressions of Godself. No human work, however polished, will fully address the work that God has already done, but all work in Christian assembly, offered faithfully unto God, can be an occasion to encounter God's Word.

Right worship reflects rhythms of work and leisure. In worship, we can rest from our labors, know that work is not our end purpose, and trust that God is already at work for us. At the beginning of the workweek Christians joyfully celebrate that our work is relative to the larger purposes of the triune God. Yet worship itself reflects something of the labors from which we rest: human actions, human offerings given to one another and offered to God. This juxtaposition of work and rest within worship frames the value of work quite honestly: work is neither uplifted as destiny nor disparaged as irrelevant to communion with God. Good work, in this sense, reflects the pace of work and rest in Christian assembly. Neither leisure alone nor work alone suffices, but when God's work informs our rest and God's rest informs our work, we participate in the good life. In worship, we see that God shuns neither work nor rest, but takes them both, blesses them, and uses them as occasions to address God's people. The Lord of the Sabbath hallows each day of the week, calling us in worship to become participants in work that gives rest and rest that informs work.

EUCHARISTIC TRANSFORMATION OF (WORK) PLACE

In an increasingly secular culture, the term "sacred" conveys a sense of a quaint, bygone era. When most, if not all, places in the world can be regarded as mundane, predictable, and devoid of mystery, sacred space disappears. In an atmosphere of secularization, one tendency among Christians has been to reserve special places as holy, distinguishing them from the workaday world. If secularism has crowded out the sacred, then Christians need to reclaim it: what is special and holy belongs to God, and what is everyday belongs to us. Christian liturgy, however, disrupts the separation of sacred and profane accelerated by secularism and countenanced by many churches. As we break bread and drink wine together, Christians do not simply set aside a special place as holy; we remember that God extends holiness to the world in all places, transforming our sense of sacred space. Some of the most significant reflections on this theme have emerged from high church traditions, those traditions that one might first expect to emphasize the sacredness of ecclesial space over against the secular.

The liturgical focus in the remaining sections of this chapter turns toward the Lord's Supper, suggesting that it offers a recapitulation of Christian liturgy. In giving thanks, offering gifts, confessing sin, and receiving the promise of Christ's body and blood given for the world, Christians celebrate at table the movements of God's grace for the world. Though not the summation of Christian liturgy, the Eucharist does embody its chief movements. In this sacrament, amid the sacred things at table, in the sacred time and place of Christian assembly, Christians celebrate the presence of the risen Christ, who is at work *everywhere*, transcending the bounds of the particular time, things, and space at the Lord's Table. The Eucharist marks God's transformation of ordinary time, place, and things as they are caught up in God's life for the world. We do not leave sacred space when we rise from the table, but are opened anew to the One who is at the center of all "profane" space. The Eucharist re-members that, in Christ, ordinary space has already been transformed as Christ infuses our daily work.

In his extended meditation on the Eucharist, Alexander Schmemann offers a vision of a celestial banquet where the boundaries between sacred and profane dissipate. As Christians partake in the body and blood of Christ, they do not merely anticipate communion with the Creator, they experience that communion in the present as the source of cosmic life. The assembly of God's people is "the gathering together of heaven and earth and all creation in Christ."[12] In one sense, Christians leave profane space by entering the assembly: the sanctuary is no ordinary room; the altar no ordinary table. But when we eat bread and drink wine in this space, we are reminded that the sacred always occurs in the midst of the profane: bread and wine become body and blood; a house built with human hands becomes God's dwelling. As we approach the Table to celebrate the Eucharist, Schmemann says, we recall that "the entire world was created as an 'altar of God,' as a temple, as a symbol of the kingdom. According to its conception, it is all *sacred* and not 'profane,' for its essence lies in the divine 'very good' of Genesis."[13] In this assembly made up of beggars and wealthy persons, male and female, young and old, from across the street and around the globe, we encounter the God who makes all places God's own.

Joseph Cardinal Ratzinger echoes Schmemann in his claim that the liturgy tears open heaven and earth and "we are incorporated in the great chorus of praise."[14] In an earthly celebration we encounter the liturgy of heaven, the work of God's very hands. Ratzinger's point can easily be twisted or exaggerated so that the work of the people becomes indistinguishable from God's work.

Reformed Christianity, as it emphasizes the radical otherness of God's work, is warranted in its suspicion of liturgical theologies that may blur God's work with our own. Nonetheless, his suggestion that "heaven is torn open" is staggering in its implication for our construal of sacred places and offers an expression of radical immanence often absent from Reformed Christianity. If the breaking of bread and drinking of cup offer an intimation of heavenly liturgy, then the sacred place of the world is the world itself. Boundaries between what belongs to God and what does not disappear; God embraces all places as God reconciles the world to Godself. God's pursuit of us in profane space, in other words, is relentless; there is no place on earth where we can escape this reconciling work. "Where can I go from your spirit? Or where can I flee from your presence? If I ascend to heaven, you are there; if I make my bed in Sheol, you are there" (Ps. 139:7–8).

The Eucharist, in its sacred use of ordinary things among ordinary people, subverts our desire to carve out space that is ours alone. Such longings are false, because all space belongs to God. As the One who cannot be grasped by his disciples, the risen Christ penetrates all spaces.[15] If we see in the liturgy of Christian assembly the movement of God's life for the world, then we should expect Christ's presence to crop up continually, even in the midst of the profane. The incarnation itself reminds us that God claims and blesses the profane—the trade of carpentry, the life of a colonized Jew—as God's own. Few theologians have recognized the implications of this claim as poetically as Pierre Teilhard de Chardin: "God, in all that is most living and incarnate in him, is not far away from us, altogether apart from the world we see, touch, hear, smell and taste about us. Rather he awaits us every instant in our action, in the work of the moment. There is a sense in which he is at the tip of my pen, my spade, my brush, my needle—of my heart and of my thought."[16] To live as eucharistic people means that we encounter the risen Christ when we write, when we dig, when we paint, and when we sew. For Teilhard, we do not celebrate the Lord's Supper to remain ensconced in ecclesial space; rather, our celebration flows out into the profane and ordinary. The Eucharist "must invade my life. My life must become, as a result of the sacrament, an unlimited and endless contact with you."[17] In the space of a simple meal, the Eucharist hallows all space and all lives caught up in its rhythms.

The practical implications of these reflections on space for a theology of work are enormous. No longer can the workplace be glimpsed as an arena foreign to the holiness of Christian faith. The work that we do and the places where we do it are claimed and blessed by the God who offers Godself in bread and wine of ordinary assembly. In liturgical space, the ordinary becomes extraordinary. The workplace is sacred not merely because Christians happen to be working in that place. Rather, the workplace is holy because "heaven has been torn open" in the liturgy, and God's holy space envelops what we think is ours alone. The workplace has value, in other words, because it too is God's place, where one cannot do work that belongs to oneself alone. Wherever work is shared and offered for the good of the people, there we encounter God at work in God's place. The Lord of Sabbath is always already at work, transforming places we think are secular into the holy ground of the Christ who encompasses all space.

These eucharistic reflections also call us to reject the ways in which we manipulate, commodify, and exploit space, as if land were for the sake of profit alone. Because there is no rigid separation between sacred and profane, a eucharistic people holds all land as God's gift. The space we inhabit, the places where we work belong not to us, but to God. Good work, then, requires the sharing of space rather than its hoarding or exploitation. Gordon Lathrop meditates on the familiar narrative of Moses at the burning bush: "When the burning, all-holy God comes, a simple location in the earth, a simple living thing—a bush—suffices for a meeting place. That unpretentious place then becomes the center of a cosmos, a world now held into the possibility of order by the attention of God."[18] This ordinary place becomes holy ground, given and claimed by God, extended to the whole world. We cannot claim the space where God meets us—whether at work or at rest; whether in solemn assemblies or a rain forest or around the foundry fire—at the expense of others. Every place is holy; only when we believe them ordinary are we capable of hoarding them like commodities that cannot be shared. When we share space as eucharistic people, however, our perception of time changes as well.

EUCHARISTIC TRANSFORMATION
OF (WORKING) TIME

Most Americans are hard-pressed for time, wishing that the day contained just a few more hours. Between demands of work, family, and other commitments, there seems to be little time to rest. In our fast-paced world, we want more time, but time keeps slipping away. This lack of time has affected even our sleep patterns, as we sleep significantly less on average than previous generations. Arlie Hochschild has observed that working mothers speak of sleep like starving people speak of food.[19] Time marches on, while the commitments of modern life gobble up more and more time. The work-saving technologies of the new millennium, such as e-mail, teleconferencing, and even "family-friendly" workplaces, blur distinctions between work and home. If I can take a child to work, then I am more likely to log long hours there; if I can take e-mail home with me, domestic space becomes an extension of the office. This maddening rush is exhausting, compressing our days, confusing our sense of place; no wonder that many of us long for the liturgical space of church as a time refuge, where we can be renewed in the midst of sacred time.[20]

As valuable as retreat and renewal are for overworked persons, the movements of the Eucharist do not simply foster an escape from frenzied time. Eucharistic time reorients us in the midst of ordinary time. For a eucharistic people, worship signals not a retreat, but a revitalization of our working days as Christians worship on the first day of the week. When we worship, moreover, we release our feverish tendency to control time, and receive it more gratefully as a gift, formed by the movements of God's time.

The time when Christians gather to worship is, in itself, significant. Very early in Christian practice, so early that it cannot be determined precisely when it began, Christians gathered on the first day of the week to celebrate the risen Lord. Gordon Lathrop reflects on the meaning of Sunday worship:

> Christians originally did not establish a new Sabbath, their own holy day and their own structuring of the week. Through Christian history the day of meeting has certainly been dealt with that way, as if the observance of the day were a new religious institution. But at the origin, when the first day was another work day, and in continuing intention, it is not so. Rather, the old beloved week still exists and, juxtaposed to it, there is the Christian meeting. It is as if the meeting were after the week, beyond the week, free of the week, and opening to a thing the week cannot contain.[21]

Christian worship does not simply occur as a pause at the end of the week; rather, it begins the week, the time that we have, by announcing good news to the world for all time. Christian worship both occurs in the midst of ordinary time, at the beginning of the workweek (and originally on an actual day of work) and beyond time, as God breaks into an ordinary day and promises communion to a time-starved and often bread-starved people. The situating of Christian worship at the beginning of the week both hallows the rest of the week and points to a holiness that is beyond our attempt to fix it to certain times.

One of the pathologies of time-crunched individuals is the desire to control time. If we feel assaulted by the demands on our time, then an understandable response is to render time an object that I can manipulate at my convenience. Innocuous personal accessories, such as watches, are but subtle reminders of our burning obsession with time. We need to know what time it is, how much time we've spent on a certain task, how much longer before we can go home. Add the watch to the multiple calendars, appointment books, personal data assistants, and e-mails that codify time, and answering machines that specify a time of call, and we assume that we manage time rather easily.

The patterns of the Eucharist, however, suggest that time is not for our manipulation or management, but given to us excessively. The words of institution invite us to remember both a distant time and a time that is ours: "We give you thanks that the Lord Jesus, on the night before he died, took bread, and after giving thanks to you, he broke it and gave it to his disciples."[22] These words draw us into a story that gives life to a broken world. We are invited back in time to remember the last meal Jesus shared with his disciples, and are promised that the same Host is present at table right here, in our time. The risen Christ cannot be manipulated or constrained by time, but transcends time itself. As often as we eat this bread and drink this cup, we proclaim his coming for all time. Eucharistic time, in other words, suggests that time is not placed on us as a demand, but given as a gift. All the time that we have—at work, at play, in worship, in struggle, in joy—is God's time.

In the face of our desire to control time, eucharistic time suggests at least two things for our understanding of work: first, there will always be a place to step outside of time, as it were, and be caught up in the last meal of Jesus. As we remember the night in which Jesus was betrayed, we pause from our work time and are formed by the One who works for us. The purpose of human life is not to work without end, but to exist in communion with each other and the Creator, a communion that is possible because of the work of Jesus Christ. To re-member this, we must pause from our labors.

Second, however, eucharistic time encourages us to see our daily work as infused by Christ, the Lord of time. As we re-member the words of institution, we are not transported back in time or teleported out of time, but firmly located in the midst of the time we are given. By celebrating the Eucharist, heralding the risen Christ, we recognize that the time of work also belongs to Christ in the Holy Spirit. In the Orthodox liturgy, the anaphora signals the transformation of the eucharistic elements accomplished through the epiclesis, the prayer invoking the Holy Spirit.[23] As Christians are formed by liturgy, we might then say that as the celebration of the Lord's Supper extends to ordinary time, we recognize our lives and work as animated by the Holy Spirit. The work that we do is made possible through work that does not belong to us alone.

Christian liturgy does not attempt to control time, but to be formed by God's salvation that occurs in the midst of ordinary time. *Heilgeschichte* always occurs in time: a covenant established with a displaced people ages ago, the coming of the Redeemer in the flesh to live for thirty-odd years, the promise of creation's fulfillment at the end of time. Salvation, for Christians, does not occur by escaping time, but by being formed by God as time marches on. The liturgical calendar, then, is not a calendar upon which we schedule events, but the remembering of God's saving acts in time, and our incorporation in that story. As the church celebrates Advent, Christmas, Lent, Easter, Pentecost, and ordinary time, it is drawn into the grand narrative of time that began long before we arrived and will continue long after we have left. In the small amount of time that God gives us, we become a part of the story of creation, covenant, redemption, and consummation that God narrates in the midst of time. As we become a part of that narrative, we realize that time is not something that we can control, but that time comes as gift, surprising us in the midst of the everyday.

This intersection of liturgical and working time means that there is such a thing as enough in this story. For an overworked society, this limit to time and work appears both as relief and a disruption of our frenzied pace. To be formed by the narrative of God's time, one must let go of the attempt to control time and the tendency to cram more work into less time for the sake of efficiency. We can work too much in the scope of the narrative, whenever our work deafens us to the story itself. When work becomes an end in itself, it has consumed too much of our time.

Liturgical narratives encourage us to live all our moments out of God's time. Whether we work or whether we play, we are living from the Spirit, the Lord and Giver of Life. One of the first tests of good work, then, is what kind of attitude it produces toward time. Does our work encourage us to see time as a scarce commodity or demand more out of us in less time? Does working time overwhelm time for rest? Does work encourage me to see others as constraints on time? Answering affirmatively to any of these questions suggests that the rhythms of a workplace are out of sync with the narrative of God's time. Good work, by contrast, sees time as a gift, and encourages the extension of that gift to others: where the time that I spend working redounds to others' enjoyment of the time they are given. When time is enjoyed and embraced as gift, that narrative becomes contagious, for it is the only narrative capable of giving life, even in the midst of material prosperity.

EUCHARISTIC THINGS AND THINGS OF LIFE AND WORK

A mantra that reverberates in consumer culture is that we work to secure an abundance of things. The rewards of good work are not found in the knowledge of work well done, but in the host of prizes that result from hard work. If we work hard enough, we too can possess a house that is the envy of our neighbors, a car that meshes with our lifestyle, technological gadgets to soothe our ennui, and a big-screen television to saturate us with advertising and the desire for yet more things. The elusive promise of consumer society is that these things make us happy. Even if our work proves a grind, the things we buy because of work will satisfy our hunger. In this atmosphere, the Eucharist offers another perspective. Acquiring things will only increase our restlessness and dissatisfaction; when God blesses the work of our hands, however, we are drawn back to the basic things of life: bread shared with the world, labor shared with others, the fruits of labor shared in abundance. Only these basic things of life can truly satisfy: bread, work that is cooperative, communion with each other and God. The Lord's Supper fixes our attention on these things, blesses the human work involved in their creation, and calls us to share them with others.

Our consumer society is materialistic, in the sense that it encourages the rapid consumption of material things. The eucharistic milieu is also materialist, but in another sense: the Eucharist reminds us that God embraces, blesses, and assumes the material as a vehicle of encounter with God's very self. The Bible is filled with narratives of God's preference for the material: creating a material cosmos for relationship with the creator; establishing an earthly covenant with a decidedly imperfect people; the incarnation of God's son in the flesh; his resurrection of the body; the establishment of the church, the Body of Christ, for the world. The Eucharist recapitulates these movements in its remembrance of Christ's body broken for the world and blood shed for it. As Nicholas Apostola has written, "The economy of God employs matter for spiritual ends, and thus sanctifies it."[24] This employment of matter, properly spoken, is Christian materialism, a marked departure from consumerist materialism. Whereas consumerism encourages us to devour matter and use up as much as possible, Christian materialism teaches us to preserve and value the material as claimed and blessed by God. In the Eucharist, matter is neither discarded nor destroyed, but taken up into God's very life. Christian materialism reminds us that the things of life are basic: bread, blood, water, flesh, and work.[25]

Lathrop echoes this vision of Christian materialism in his meditation on the ordinary food of the Lord's Supper: "Bread represents the earth and the rain, growing grains, sowing and reaping, milling and baking, together with the mystery of yeast, all presented in a single object."[26] This staple of human life, this food that is consumed more regularly by more people across culture than anything else—whether in the form of a corn tortilla, potato latke, French baguette, or Ethiopian sponge bread—is what God takes and blesses as holy. Wine, likewise, is a basic thing, more festive than most other beverages. Convivial, life-enhancing, even dangerous if overconsumed, wine shows us that food and drink not only nourish, but exhilarate. The basic food of sustenance and the basic drink of celebration hold central place at the Lord's Table, reminding us that God is no stranger to the basic meals that sustain and celebrate human life.

These elements of the meal remind us that God is no stranger to work. The central items at the Lord's Table are not wheat and grapes, the raw stuff God gives us, but bread and wine, the products of human labor. Countless hours—indeed, years—of work go into the bread that appears at the Lord's Table each Sunday: tilling soil at the beginning of planting season, sowing seed preserved from last year, watering nascent plants, weeding seedlings, praying for sufficient sun and rain, harvesting grain when it is ripe and golden, threshing wheat from chaff, grinding wheat into flour, mixing flour into dough, stirring in yeast, baking the loaf, bringing bread to market, to say nothing of the hours of planning, research, and transportation involved in each of these steps. The wine, likewise, is the product of endless hours of cultivation, trimming, pressing, fermentation, bottling, and marketing. Vineyards, moreover, do not produce an immediate yield, but require years of labor before even the first fruits appear. These holy things of bread and wine are the products of human hands applied to the bounty God has given; they are there because we work.[27] Without human labor, there is no Eucharist.

Our work alone, however, does not secure the place of these holy things. The bread and the wine also represent, in Lathrop's words, "the cooperation of human work with the land."[28] God gives us rains that water the earth, soil that nourishes the seedling, sun that radiates upon the land. Work the land too much, and it will yield no more; plant water-intensive plants in regions of the earth where water is scarce, and wells become depleted. The good work of human hands is *cooperative* labor, attending closely to the needs of the land. In a manner that hearkens Israel's Sabbath practice, good work looks for a sustainable yield rather than the absolute maximum. Good work does not control or master the land, but considers the land as coworker. Exploit this coworker, and bread becomes scarcer and wine more costly.

When our work attends the rhythms of God's creation, we encounter the mystery of God's incarnational presence in the midst of our ordinary days. Teilhard describes this mystery vividly: "Right from the hands that knead the dough, to those that consecrate it, the great and universal Host should be prepared and handled in a spirit of *adoration*."[29] The everyday human labors of kneading and baking, cultivation and pressing, are labors that God claims as God's own in Jesus Christ. Eucharistic time encourages us to attend to all work in a similar spirit of reverence. Our work does not create anything solely on its own, but when it responds to the work God has already done—when it mirrors, however fleetingly and incompletely, the attentiveness of divine work—then our work, too, can bring about things of beauty and wonder. Work of this kind seeks not itself, but others.

At the risk of exaggeration, such work also seeks the universe. Good work is consistently cognizant of its dependence on others, on the cosmos itself, and on the Lord of Creation. When we present the bread and wine on the table, the products of our labor, God takes them, blesses them, and gives us life. To our small response, God gives us God's very self over and again. Our offering becomes God's gift to us. Schmemann writes, "That is why it is not 'simply' bread that lies on the diskos. On it all of God's creation is presented, manifested in Christ as the new creation, the fulfillment of the glory of God."[30] Many contemporary attitudes toward work see human labor (and the fruits of human labor) as a zero-sum game. In order for me to have a job, someone else must be out of work; in order for my family to secure enough bread to live, some others must invariably go without. I must, therefore, compete with others for employment that is scarce and things that are even dearer. The eucharistic economy, however, reveals work that redounds to creation and others, rather than taking away from them. Work can be shared, the fruits of labor can multiply as God continues to give Godself in our offerings; goods need not only be private.[31] To a disaffected populace, such work satisfies.

This work satisfies because its bounty is shared among many. In contrast to fruits of work that we "earn" for ourselves, the food of the Eucharist is public, given for all. As Meister Eckhardt once claimed, "There is no such thing as 'my' bread. All bread is ours and given to me, to others through me, and to me through others."[32] Having partaken of this holy meal, sharing in Christ's body and blood, we rise from table to share this meal and ourselves with the world. It is no coincidence that offerings for the poor accompany celebrations of Holy Communion; without giving and sharing, the meal devolves into gluttony. We come to the Lord's Table hungry, responding to God's work with tokens of our labor in bread and wine; God takes these elements, blesses them, and gives us Godself, nourishing and satisfying our hungry hearts. Yet we leave the table not sated, but yearning for this food to be shared with all, recognizing that the reign of God is not yet among us, that injustice suppurates in all corners of the globe, that thousands die every day for lack of daily bread. Nourished at the Lord's Table, we also go away hungry, rising from this meal to share ourselves and our bread with others.

M. Shawn Copeland has claimed that hunger constitutes "a possibility for discipleship. If we would be disciples of Jesus, we must be willing to recognize and alleviate hungers whether for Eucharist or food or truth or justice, whether our own hungers or those of others."[33] When work is hoarded, hunger increases as famine; fed at the Lord's Table, shared work intensifies our hunger for righteousness and justice so that our work issues forth in bread for the world. Good work satisfies because it is caught up in God's labor for the world, seeking to extend God's bounty to all; but this same work leaves us restless when we recognize that many do not partake in that abundance. A mix of hunger and satisfaction, therefore, characterize the Christian journey into the reign of God. As our thirst is quenched and hunger satisfied every time we eat and drink at the Lord's Table, we hunger that God's reign will come. Hungering, we also know it is already here, summoning our response and our work on behalf of the kingdom, where all things, basic and holy, are shared.[34]

The satisfaction that the Eucharist offers the world is different from the abundance of things promised by an American work ethic. Amid the holy things at table, we are reminded that only the basic stuff of life, shared in the fellowship of others, is what truly satisfies. Fulfillment is not found in work that constantly seeks more things, but in work that acknowledges its insufficiency but offers itself nonetheless. When we respond to God's grace, we come to the table empty-handed, offering in bread and wine tokens of our labor, desiring that they, too, might be shared. When we respond in this manner, we hunger and thirst for justice and righteousness, not simply for more things. The holy things at table turn our attention squarely to others. As Richard Gaillardetz notes, "We find human fulfillment precisely when we cease making fulfillment the immediate end of all our actions and instead give ourselves over freely to lives of committed service and love."[35] Such is the shape of our empty-handed, yet fulfilling work.

To a culture that revels in acquisition, these things at table are oddities indeed, for they are things that keep giving and long to be shared. Having more things, in the end, will never satisfy us; it will only deaden our hearts by inuring them to the hungers of others. Work that strives chiefly for things is work that cannot cease and soon becomes toil. Work that takes its cue from the holy things at table, however, can satisfy at the same time that it hungers for the reign of God. The dynamics of this work become clearer when we consider the Eucharist itself as gift, which equips us for gifting others.

GIFTS AT TABLE, GIFTS AT WORK

A society bent on working for things does not expect gifts and cannot accept them. As recent attempts at welfare reform have insisted, the good life comes only to those who deserve it by working hard enough. Giving simply does not enter the calculus of a society that expects hard work to reap its own rewards; nor is gift a factor in a society that assumes an acceptable level of unemployment. Work comes to those who deserve and are competent enough for it. In the exchange of the marketplace gifts are odd: on the rare occasions that they do appear, the typical response is that one should repay the giver in order to express appreciation and to stay out of the giver's debt: "In return for your kind invitation to a meal at your house, I'll bake you some cookies for dessert." Gifts easily become media of exchange, and when they do, they mirror other media:

barter, money, credit. In a eucharistic economy, however, gifts are really gifts: they expect nothing in return, but in the strange dynamic of grace, they equip the receiver to give as well. The eucharistic economy is not a zero-sum game, where only a limited number of gifts may be given away, lest the goods become exhausted. Rather, the more we receive at table, the more we are able to give ourselves. When our work gains its momentum from this economy of giving, rather than an economy of acquisition, it also can be a response to God's gift.

The Roman Catholic tradition often refers to the elements of Holy Communion as gifts and saturates the sacrament with language of gift. For the Protestant Reformers, this language was problematic, in part, because it carried overt implications that we, or the priest, were offering sacrifices to God on the altar. In the eyes of the Reformers, it was important to identify God, not ourselves, as the inaugurator of sacrifice. One can acknowledge these concerns and also lament that the language of gift has subsided in Reformed celebrations of Eucharist, as it focuses squarely on God's offer of Godself in the Supper. This language reminds us that we receive at the table the gift of the Incarnate Son, whose body is broken and blood is shed for the world. But the language of gift also suggests that in response to that divine gift, we are empowered to give something of ourselves. Communion, though it begins and ends in God, also evokes our response. The gift of the Lord's Supper inaugurates a communion of ceaseless giving that cannot be reduced to commodity exchange.

Reclaiming the language of gift, contra Reformed worries, removes us from the center of eucharistic sacrifice. At table, we are receivers, not bearers, of the gift. Schmemann depicts this dynamic rather convincingly:

> Each time we again offer this sacrifice, we know with joy that we offer it *through Jesus Christ*, that it is he who, giving himself to us and abiding in us, eternally offers the sacrifice that was once and forever offered by him. In offering our life to God, we know that we are offering Christ—for he is our life, the life of the world, and the life of life, and we have nothing to bring to God except him.[36]

We come to the table bringing nothing but ourselves: hungry, broken, longing for communion. By receiving God's very self in bread that we bake and wine that we press, we are thus able to give ourselves, knowing that in offering gifts, Christ is the offering and offerer. When we give something of ourselves, God gives back God's very self, and the gift keeps giving, inexhaustibly, irresistibly.

The gift that we receive at Table is the only thing that sustains us. Calvin writes that as bread "nourishes, sustains and keeps the life of our body, so Christ's body is the only food to invigorate and enliven our soul."[37] Yearning for life, God's gift enables us to live. Because this gift is complete, bestowing life, it points to work that we cannot accomplish on our own. Indeed, the gift at Table indicates that the main work in the world is already complete. "In Christ, everything is 'done' and no one needs to add anything to his work."[38] Receiving this gift, we know that we live by grace, and not by the dint of our own work. Freed from the manacles of trying to be self-made individuals (or individuals determined by our employers, overseers, or others who would "own" our work), we can live as receivers of the gift of life. Owing our lives to God, we respond in joy and thanks, in the freedom of gratitude rather than the compulsion of trying to please others, God, or the observers of our work.

At one level, we who have received this gift can do nothing. Graced with our lives, there is nothing we can give God in return that God does not already have. Schmemann writes, "There is nothing we can *do*, yet we become all that God wanted us to be from eternity, when we are *eucharistic*."[39] Yet we rise from the Table, depart in peace, and return to the world with the lives we have been given. The gift of life enables us to respond with joy: we leave a sanctuary and return to work in the midst of the world. When we return, our work is graced by an economy of gift.

God's giving, however, cannot be reduced to an exchange of commodities. Having received God's gift, we in turn seek to share with others. Stephen Webb writes:

> We do not give in order to receive for ourselves but in order to give something back to God who gives. Our giving is not governed by the logic of compensation and return but by the desire to follow the essential dynamic of all gifts, which is to return them to their origin, in God, by giving them to others. . . . We do not have to choose between giving to God and giving to others; by giving to others, we are participating in the momentum of God's giving, which multiplies and dispenses gifts even as they are directed to the one Giver.[40]

All that we are, all that we will be, comes from God; the divine life graces us with life itself, indicating that divine giving assumes abundance rather than scarcity. Contrary to marketplace assumptions, giving does not result in depletion, so that some have more and God has less. Rather, the divine giving operates out of a reality of *pleroma*. The more God "empties" Godself in the incarnation, the more fulfilled creation becomes in relation to God, the more the fullness of God is revealed to creation.[41] God gives not out of scarcity, but out of excess, so that the divine giving enables us to give to each other. In the divine economy, *pleroma* and *kenosis* go hand-in-hand. The former without the latter amounts to a hoarding of goods; the latter without the former devolves into self-abnegation. The gifting economy of God points to a third way, in which communion among creation and the Creator is electrified by gifts that keep on giving, goods that are shared, relationships that flourish in the midst of these gifts.

To these gifts, we cannot but respond with gratitude and gifts of our own. But we give back not to compensate for the gift we have received. Divine giving subverts tit-for-tat assumptions that permeate contemporary practices of gift exchange. By responding to God with our lives, with our labors, and with our praise and thanksgiving, we, too, offer gifts. As Gaillardetz writes, "We offer such 'return gifts,' not because the gifts can balance out the divine gift, but because the giving of a gift in return actually becomes a constitutive part of the reception and establishes communion. Indeed, this is why there is an intrinsically ethical dimension in the liturgy. The exercise of justice and mercy are essential dimensions of our return gift."[42] The holy things at Table are tokens of God's gift to the world; we give not to render ourselves out of the debt of the Giver, but because we respond out of God's fullness, even in our poverty. "God acts, and, empty-handed, we respond to God's goodness in a 'sacrifice of praise and thanksgiving.' "[43] The giving of gifts does not depend on material wealth, moral uprightness, or religious fervor; one gives because one has accepted the gift of new life and is thus empowered to keep giving.

In giving, we give what we have already been given. To glimpse this gift-giving in action we need look no further than the collection of offerings that accompany the Lord's Supper. This practice, which has been a part of Christian worship since its earliest days, is not for the maintenance of the church; it is for the poor. Having come to the table hungry, we leave it hungry on behalf of the poor. Our work in offering does not proceed because we have already secured ourselves and have sufficient reserve cash; it proceeds from the divine economy, where fulfillment and giving, *pleroma* and *kenosis*, are one and the same gift.

Gathering at the Lord's Table, we do not simply partake in Holy Communion, we embody it as we respond to God in sacrifice, thanksgiving, and praise. Augustine locates the eucharistic sacrifice not in the fraction of the priest, but in the congregation itself:

> The whole redeemed community, that is to say, the congregation and the fellowship of the saints, is offered to God as a universal sacrifice, through the great Priest who offered himself in his suffering for us— so that we might be the body of so great a head. . . . This is the sacrifice which the Church continually celebrates in the sacrament of the altar, a sacrament well-known to the faithful where it is shown to the Church that she herself is offered in the offering which she presents to God.[44]

Metaphors for Communion throughout theological traditions—from Paul to Augustine to Luther to liberation and feminist theologians—have been decidedly corporeal. Gaining life from Christ's body given to us, we become ourselves part of that body as we are animated by him as the head and sustained by the breath of the Holy Spirit. Fed at Table, we respond in communion with one another. The gifts we receive always find others.

If our daily work draws its sustenance from the divine gift, then it also recognizes the unique gifts of God's people. Though God dispenses the gift of life to all indiscriminately, the contours of our response to that gift are unique. Paul describes these responses as gifts (*charisma*) granted by the Spirit: some are given the gift of teaching, others healing, still others prophecy and leadership (1 Cor. 12). Good work fosters the development of each of these gifts. In a society that settles for substandard schools in poorer neighborhoods, in an economy that places the costs of higher education increasingly out of reach for hundreds of thousands of young people, in a nation that maintains an acceptable level of unemployment, the gifts of all cannot flourish. Good work allows gifts to increase, so that we can express ourselves through our work and thereby give to others. Taking the rhythms of the Lord's Table to heart, our work can be an expression of our truest selves: persons gifted with life by God who give to others. When an artist paints, she offers an interpretation of the world, expresses herself, gives to others, and praises God with her brush. When an accountant carefully tabulates expense sheets and keeps budgets so that a shipping company can transport wheat from one end of the Pacific to another, he employs his gift with mathematics, gives it to others, and in no small manner gives thanks to God. When a janitor vacuums a classroom floor so that children can sit on the carpet for story time, she expresses a gift for detail, gives to children and teacher, and responds to the God who makes us a part of God's story. As each of these workers gives to others, those who receive them are better equipped to pass on their unique gifts. Gifts at table keep on giving.

This eucharistic economy of gift and communion runs counter to understandings of work that stress individualism and competition. In a eucharistic economy, there is no such thing as "my work" that I preserve at the expense of another's. In order for my work to succeed, the current mantra stresses, I need to beat out the other guy: my work and myself always take precendence. In a eucharistic economy, however, the good work of one invariably redounds to the work of another. The manufacture of high-quality computer chips by one company, for example, does not mean the demise of other chip manufacturers. Rather, the introduction of faster, more dependable chips actually accelerates the development of yet higher-quality chips. In an exclusively competitive and individualistic economy, by contrast, the end aim of chip manufacturing would be to decimate the competition and achieve monopoly status. Once the competition disappeared, moreover, hard work of design and production could abate, and eventually slow to a standstill in the absence of competitive incentives. Competitiveness and individualism by themselves prove self-destructive and wasteful, because they leave little room for the common good of work.

In contrast, gift and communion stress the importance of others and relationships between workers. The good work of one person (or manufacturer) inevitably benefits others, because the fruits of that work are shared. Good work does not feed on itself and exhaust itself, but encourages others to work well in response. Though such exhortations sound idealistic, they actually serve many industries and institutions quite well. Scientific think tanks, for example, thrive on collaborative work that stresses the relationship of one person's research to another's, as researchers constantly rely on others' work. Many of the technological advances of the last century—such as computers, immunizations, and mass transit—would have been inconceivable had individualism and competition alone dictated the work of research. Farming cooperatives employ similar measures of collaborative work, often resulting in the continued existence of sustainable agriculture and small family farms. Academic inquiry itself is well-nigh impossible without some approximation of gift and communion. The language of gift is not a pious truism; it works because it extends gifts to others so that they may give. Such giving never exhausts itself; having received the gift, we cannot help but give with our own empty hands.

EUCHARISTIC ANTICIPATION:
TRANSFORMATION OF WORK AND WORLD

At Table, Christians anticipate the reign of God that is already among us; in sharing the bread and the wine, they remember God's future.[45] Both prongs of these seemingly dissonant affirmations are crucial to Christian witness and its vision for the transformation of work. Christians anticipate the coming reign, where swords are forged into plowshares, but also know that this reign is present at the Lord's Table; the reign we anticipate is already among us. Christians remember the future as God re-members us in Holy Communion. As we anticipate the transformation of work and world in Jesus Christ, Christians do not engage in speculative prognosis, but are formed anew by the practices of the Lord's Table. Christians call the Eucharist, then, the "sacrament of the kingdom": it invites us into God's future by making us participants in God's reign, where our work is renewed over and again.

For Augustine the Eucharist represents the sacrifice of the redeemed community which receives the sacrifice of Christ. This sacrifice, for Augustine and many other church fathers, was a means of the Christian's divinization, whereby God draws the believer into deeper and fuller communion with Godself.[46]

Echoing this interpretation, John Chrysostom claims that in Holy Communion, we are united with Christ and each other: "That which when angels behold, they tremble, and dare not so much as look up at it without awe on account of the brightness that cometh thence, with this we are fed, with this we are commingled, and we are made one body and flesh with Christ."[47] In decidedly mystical language, these early theologians stressed that we become who we are, by grace, in communion. The transformation of the self is wrought not by one's own work, but through intimate relationship with the Divine, tasting and seeing that the Lord is good. The eucharistic self is always a self-in-relation-to-others, graced by God. Knowledge of the reign of God, in other words, begins with the transformation of relationships, away from multiple preoccupations (whether work- or self-oriented), toward a living and breathing with others, in and through God. Holy Communion changes us, anticipating the transformation already wrought in the world through Jesus Christ.

This foreshadowing of God's reign, moreover, reverberates beyond the interpersonal. The Eucharist is called the "sacrament of the kingdom" not merely because it results in the transformation of self, but because it embodies a reign where bread is shared, wine is poured abundantly, and all are welcomed at the banquet table. At Table, we herald a transformed world. Victor Codina writes: "The sacraments are those symbolic acts of the church that are oriented to the realization of the Kingdom of God. . . . They are particularly intense and transparent moments of the Kingdom of God in the church . . . in which the presence of the Kingdom of God is manifested as gift and as task." As task and challenge, the Eucharist announces God's reign, denounces the powers of death, and elicits our labor in the transformation of history.[48]

As God's reign summons our work, we notice a catch: the reign in which we are incorporated, for which we devote our life's labors, has already been accomplished in and through Christ. The good news of the kingdom is both that it has already come and that we must continue to labor for the rest of our lives. Feasting at Table is both a summons for our own work—to align that work with God's work for the world—and a reassurance that this work has already been done. Ambushed by the reign of God, Christians are not faced with a rigid either/or choice: either we must labor assiduously for the kingdom, or wait patiently and passively for the kingdom to come. Either position alone is a distortion of Christian ethics (with Catholics, historically, lapsing at times into the former and Protestants falling prey to the latter). The good news of Christian life is *both*: the work that we are summoned to has already been accomplished in Jesus Christ and the coming of the Holy Spirit. Therefore we rest in God's work and are summoned to work for the realization of God's reign among us. Our work is designed for participation in God's life, a work that is already done. Schmemann writes, "The liturgy is served on earth, and this means in the time and space of 'this world.' But if it is served on earth, *it is accomplished in heaven, in the new time of the new creation*, in the time of the Holy Spirit. . . . What is accomplished in heaven is already accomplished, already *is*, already *has been accomplished*, already *given*."[49] Every time Christians eat this bread and drink this cup, we proclaim his dying, rising, and coming again—work that is already accomplished at Table.

Eucharistic longing for God's reign, therefore, is not a matter of idle wish fulfillment. Though we come to the table hungry, we do not pine for a promised coming that bears no resemblance to the present. Christian eschatology, in its classic strains, stresses the radical renewal of the present order and remembrance of the past. God molds and blesses creation as good, draws creation to God's self, and annihilates nothing that God has made. The work of God's hand does not, in the end, vanish into nothingness. In the Eucharist's announcement of God's reign, we do not depart from this good creation, but "see the world in Christ, as it really is, and not from our particular and therefore limited and partial points of view."[50] To understand the world in its fullness, we need look no further than the Lord's Table: there, in abundance, is food for the world, shared among many, broken, blessed, and given for others. Our work, in other words, does not as much make the world as it participates in divine work that gives the world its life.

Some of these reflections may sound odd to some Reformed ears: a Eucharist that accomplishes a reign in heaven that is already present among us, human labor that borders on cooperation with God's work. Though these emphases are not prominent in modern Reformed worship, Calvin offers a resonant interpretation of Christ's presence in the Lord's Supper that hearkens some of these high church claims. Calvin worried that Catholic theories of transubstantiation and Lutheran attempts to ground Christ's presence in, with, and under the Supper both domesticated Christ, who had risen and was seated at the right hand of the Father. Any articulation of real presence that sought to bring Christ down to us compromised the ascension. His alternative interpretation, rather than denying real presence, affirmed it insofar as we, by the power of the Holy Spirit in the Supper, are lifted up to Christ and partake in a heavenly banquet.[51] The affirmation of real presence, for Calvin, is nothing short of our own participation in the divine life. In the meal Christ does not condescend to us as much as we are uplifted to him. The Eucharist thus entails the transformation of human life and the life of the world, for, if the Supper beckons us to heaven, we and our work are forever changed.

As eucharistic people, the effect of work already accomplished for us results in a surprising freedom in our work. Once we recognize that we belong to God, that no other person can own our work, once we are freed from the trap of reducing our identities to work, once our labors draw sustenance from the work enacted at the Lord's Table, our work becomes less our own as it is given to others. Teilhard intones, "So, gradually, the worker no longer belongs to himself. Little by little the great breath of the universe has insinuated itself into him through the fissure of his humble but faithful action, has broadened him, raised him up, borne him on."[52] Good work, in other words, comes not from inordinate attachment to one's labors, but by glimpsing those labors in and through the divine work. The sanctification of Christian life is bound up with the life of the world. At the Lord's Table, we see all—the life of individuals, the life of communities, the life of the cosmos—taken, blessed, and transformed by God.

Teilhard claims that the effects of this transformation are so pervasive that all human work, in some way, is already a response to the divine work. He reflects, "No one lifts his little finger to do the smallest task unless moved, however obscurely, by the conviction that he is contributing infinitesimally (at least indirectly) to the building of something definitive—that is to say, to your work, my God."[53] Later, in the same book, he dubs our labor as "collaborative" in "the completing of the world."[54] Teilhard's ebullience is easily refuted, especially given the cataclysmic work of the twentieth and twenty-first centuries: can the labors that spawned Hiroshima, Auschwitz, Darfur, and 9/11 be deemed collaborative with divine work? The soaring height of his rhetoric, at times, gets in the way of his theology. Yet Teilhard's point is not to argue for the divinity of all human work; much of it, in fact, is idolatrous and life-negating. His point, rather, is that the Eucharist, when celebrated, has a tendency to perpetuate itself in all kinds of work. When eucharistic people celebrate the Lord's Supper, they change, a change that surfaces in all the work they do, no matter how much they may attempt to suppress it through self-interest, greed, and mean-spiritedness. Christ's body crops up in bodies other than his own.[55]

As we are shaped by the Eucharist, nourished again and again in its celebration, we rise from the table as empty-handed as before, but equipped and impelled to respond to the work we encounter there in our uniquely empty-handed ways. When we respond in this manner, we remember that our work belongs not solely to us, but to God and to others. Though part of the creation of self, work is also part of the transformation of the world and our relationships with others. But our work creates and transforms only because God is already at work, transforming us and our world. The Eucharist is performative—proclaiming and embodying a reign that is already among us, a work that is already accomplished. Yet it is also exhortative—summoning our work for a reign that has not yet arrived. When we rise from the table we are still hungry and yearn for those hungers to cease. The fact that hunger will not cease in time is no excuse not to work. Indeed, they make our labors all the more crucial, given the short time we have. What keeps us from exhausting ourselves in that work are the promises we encounter at Table: God's work is already taken, blessed, broken, and given to us. These gestures of God's work form a vision for the transformation of our own labors.

GESTURES OF GOOD WORK

"While they were eating, Jesus took a loaf of bread, and after blessing it he broke it, gave it to the disciples, and said, 'Take, eat; this is my body' " (Matt. 26:26). With nearly identical words, each of the Synoptic Gospels records Jesus' gestures and sayings as he shares bread and wine with his disciples during their final meal together. They are words and gestures that recall his feeding of the five thousand (Matt. 14:19; Mark 6:41; Luke 9:16), words and gestures that resound with celebrations of Passover. Jesus *takes, blesses, breaks,* and *gives*: what he does with the bread, he also does with his life. In this final meal, Jesus' actions capture the pattern of his work for the world: gestures of grace given for many.[56] What Jesus does with his life and with this food, he gives to the world. The rhythms of his actions at Table offer a window for how we might envision good work.

Jesus takes the bread; Jesus takes his life. He gathers before himself the food on hand: rather ordinary bread, the kind that people in his culture ate every day. But in his gesture of grace, this ordinary loaf becomes his body. Jesus takes his life, the life of a first-century Palestinian Jew living under the reign of Caesar, a life of a man who worked with his hands, a life of a man who struggled against systems that fostered self-righteousness and acquiescence to poverty and injustice. But in this ordinary life, we encounter the decisive inbreaking of God. Jesus takes what he has been given and transforms it to reflect the radiant, sustaining presence of God. All that Jesus is given is from God; he takes it and directs it back to God.

Good work also takes what we have been given. The Holy Spirit has graced each worker, each person, with gifts that no other person can replicate. To be sure, these gifts require constant cultivation: Mozart's gift for music was only honed to good use through diligent practice, but this practice became artful because of Mozart's unique gifts. Practicing scales as Mozart did does not guarantee that one will play and compose as he did. The world is richer, for example, that Nelson Mandela did *not* practice as much as Mozart, but cultivated his gifts for leadership instead. Discerning particular gifts is one of the first steps in forming a vision of good work. Work that fulfills, work that expresses some response to the work God has already done, requires that we take the gifts we have been given.

Standards of teaching, for example, that do not allow for teachers to cultivate their gifts will fail this criterion of good work. When elementary school curricula become so programmed and rigid that each minute of the day is marked for subjects that can only be taught in a specified manner, then education becomes less the practice and nurture of gifts and more force-feeding of information to passive vessels. Good work of teaching, by contrast, accounts for difference in teaching and learning styles. Some will teach elementary students through stories; others through building projects; others through music. Good work will allow for the cultivation of a variety of gifts unique to each child in the classroom. A one-size-fits-all approach to teaching and learning both minimizes the mystery that is at the heart of education and stifles the gifts each student and teacher have been given. Good work takes these gifts and allows them to express themselves.

Jesus blesses: he gives thanks to God for the bread and blesses the loaf, responding to the gifts God has given. Jesus blesses everything he touches; no person or thing is too tainted for his touch. Jesus' table fellowship is staggering in that he will eat with *anyone*: beggars, outcasts, prostitutes, tax collectors, even those who seek to kill him. To eat with someone is to convey a blessing, to offer a gesture of hospitality and thanks dearer than almost any other gesture. Jesus eats with others to feed the hungry and gladden the hearts of those gathered around the table. As he subverts bounds of social association and ritual cleanness, Jesus shows us that all people are recipients of God's blessing. For each one of them, Jesus gives thanks.

Good work is also blessed. If Jesus' touch extended to all, it doubtless includes daily work. In his own life, Jesus shows us how seemingly mundane work is taken, claimed, and blessed by God. Gaillardetz reminds us that before his public ministry, Jesus of Nazareth

> practiced a trade and, following the death of his father, took care of a family . . . The incarnation affirms that God is to be discovered in a world filled with mundane daily tasks for which few are canonized: the world of family and work, the world of daily labor, meal preparation, and household chores. He took all that is ordinary and, to our modern eyes, boring and without value, and he blessed it and made it holy.[57]

Good work recognizes that God's blessing touches all work. In Jesus of Nazareth's assumption of the flesh, he renders work blessed. All tasks that human beings do to maintain, cultivate, create, and observe their world are taken by the life of the Redeemer and oriented to the Holy.

Blessing also implies another sense: good work also is an expression of thanks. If all work is claimed and blessed by God, then our response is to echo that blessing in thanksgiving. Good work, in other words, is not a burden to be borne, but an occasion for expressing one's thanks to the Creator of all gifts. When I am gifted with unique abilities and aptitudes, when God blesses the work that utilizes those gifts, I respond by giving thanks, both in word and action. Good work, in and of itself, is an expression of thanks: a finely crafted chair, a graceful gymnastics routine, a sound medical diagnosis, a brightly waxed car, all involve work that employs gifts and gives thanks for them. Indeed, as an expression of thanks, the work of our hands often speaks more clearly and distinctly than our words.

Good work acknowledges God's blessing of all labor and allows for expressions of thanks. Ample work exists, however, that does not correspond to either of these dimensions. Mind-numbing work, for example, smothers thanks instead of giving it voice. Work owned by others squashes individual gifts rather than fostering them. Taylorist assembly-line methods, which compartmentalize work so rigidly that one worker is given the task of fastening one screw in the same place—widget after endless widget—deaden the heart and our capacity for giving thanks. Work of these types neither cultivates the unique gifts of individuals nor expresses the blessing that God is the endower of all life, for to give thanks, we must be able to express the whole of ourselves, and not wear ourselves thin by overexerting one of our capacities.

Even assembly-line work, however, can become an expression of thanks so long as workers are not reduced to the particular roles they occupy in the line. Recent attempts to integrate assembly-line workers into factory governance decisions, for example, recognize that all workers express gifts and thanks. At best, they recognize that those closest to machine work provide distinctly needed voices in framing the work of the factory as a whole.[58] In these models, the assembly-line worker is always more than the particular task she or he is summoned to do. One criterion for whether work is an expression of blessing, then, is whether it allows for the expression of more than one isolated task. Blessing, as it envelops all of life, elicits a response of the whole person.

Jesus breaks bread. The bread that he breaks feeds the hungry; bread that he gives as his own body is broken because of the world and for the world. Jesus is the One who is both broken by the world on account of sin and the one who breaks himself for the world to forgive sin. His body bears the scars of a crown of thorns and the pierce of a spear. His body, brokenhearted and broken-boned, is given for others. Jesus' brokenness cannot be reduced, however, to the wounds that a sinful world inflicts on him. Brokenness, to be sure, is a mark of sin, but the breaking of Jesus' body also makes communion possible. We enter into communion with Christ in his willing breaking of himself. The breaking of his body is an opening for the world. In breaking himself, Jesus renders himself not simply his own, as if his body were his alone. As his body is broken, it is given for the world. To break bread is to share it, not to hoard it to oneself. Jesus does the very same thing with his body, a body given for the life of the world.

This double valence of breaking carries over to a vision of good work. All human work is broken as it is scarred by sin. No work of our hands offers an unadulterated glimpse of godly work. Sermons that proclaim the word of God become occasions for ego stroking and self-aggrandizement. Powerful athletic feats become occasions for greed and cult of celebrity. Songs that express the longings of the human heart are co-opted as advertising jingles for gas-guzzling SUVs. The most egregious examples of sin infesting work are relatively easy to spot, but no work is immune from sin's cancer. Even if sin permeates our work, however, this does not negate the great good that comes from flawed labor. As the incarnation demonstrates, as the history of the church documents, God brings treasure out of earthen vessels. Indeed, recognizing sin on its own terms frees us from justifying ourselves through work and to name good work when we see it. This recognition of sin within work also serves as a reminder that work is not the proper end of human beings. Though we are made to work, endless work is not our lot. We are, rather, to enjoy communion with God and each other forever. Yet as sin breaks the body of Christ, so, too, does it break our work.

Good work is also broken in the sense that we render it open to others. Jesus breaks bread to share with his disciples. If bread is not broken, it cannot be distributed. Good work, too, bears the traces of these seams—broken open so that others are invited in. One paradox of the Eucharist is this: in breaking, we are made whole. As bread is fragmented, the body of Christ draws together. Work that is broken open no longer belongs to itself or to a single worker, but to the whole world. Our work becomes whole, too, as it is broken for others, as the work of one draws on the work of many.

If all work is characterized by sin, only good work is broken open for others. Examples of the brokenness of sin without the breaking open of work are abundant. Bookkeeping practices that stress secrecy, protection of assets at all costs, and lack of public knowledge are examples of work hoarded to oneself. Under the guise of privacy, bookkeeping of this sort typically clings to resources at all costs, as if the fruits of work dissipate as they move beyond a close orbit of familiars and fellow beneficiaries. Recent corporate scandals document all too well this insidious tendency among American work patterns.

Good work, however, breaks open the public-private split in business practice. Its accounting and bookkeeping become a matter of public good, not private privilege. As work is broken open, the goods of the firm are shared—among employees who labor daily, among management that charts directions for the future, among stockholders who invest, and among the larger public as profits are taxed. Good work recognizes that no work can belong to itself long and flourish. Good work, rather, proliferates as it is broken open for others, as others participate in the work given. One mark of good work is whether its products and practices are broken open for others or guarded as loot.

Having taken, blessed, and broken the bread, Jesus gives it to his disciples. As Jesus gives the bread, so, too, he gives himself for the world. Bread broken is bread given. Jesus, the Broken One, gives the gift of life to Lazarus, of companionship to Mary Magdalene, of healing to lepers, of fellowship to Zacchaeus, of his life on a cross, of his resurrected body to the world. In the life of Jesus, new life is found not in clinging to oneself, but when life is given for others. The bread that Jesus gives at Table sustains a world in abundance.

Good work, likewise, gives to others and rests not in itself. When work is guarded so that others will not benefit, the result may be temporary prosperity for the hoarder, but death for a life that results in hoarding. The well-documented abuses of Enron executives offer a foil to work that is given for others. The slogan of these higher-ups was to accumulate at all costs: hoarding the proceeds of hard work and lying to stockholders, employees, and accountants in the name of good business. These executives sought to keep for themselves the proceeds of their own work without accounting for the work of others or the claim of the public upon them. As a result, pensions evaporated, stockholders lost millions, and a titan of industry crumbled while its executives profited until the end. Hoarded work leads not only to the diminishment of others' work, it also proves unsustainable in the end, because the appetite of hoarding is insatiable. Once we hoard, we can never have enough, but always something more to gain at others' expense. Work then appears as a zero-sum game in which only a few can win and others must lose. Such practices serve not to increase material abundance, but to decrease it, concentrating wealth in increasingly fewer hands.

Good work, by contrast, is given to others and results in increased abundance. One example of work given to others is found in the seeming drudgery of garbage collection. Sanitation workers are public servants. Their work is good not because it is hoarded to themselves, but because it is given to others. The collection of garbage allows the work of others to flourish. Without workers occupied with garbage collection, little in civic life could flourish: teaching, governing, policing, building. The sanitation of a town or city is the work that garbage collectors give to the public. This gift to others, moreover, increases the abundance of the city in which they work. The good work of the few involved in garbage collection invariably redounds to the good work of others. Garbage collection is but one example of good work, though it can also be done poorly, as when collection is haphazard or when recyclable materials are dumped with other waste. All work that sustains community, however, can offer analogous expressions of giving: bus mechanics who offer their services so that others may ride to work; writers whose work displays talent and also piques the conscience and heart of a people; teachers whose gift is that others might come to learn more of the world's abundance; lawyers who represent juvenile offenders; accountants who form ledger sheets so that companies continue to stay in business; backyard gardeners who give their produce to neighbors. Good work does not rest in itself, but is broken open and given to the world.

As Christians celebrate the Eucharist, we recall Christ's work in the Spirit for the world. When workers approach the Lord's Table, they first remember Christ's work. As they are transformed by his work, however, their work, too, can draw on the gestures of the Supper. In the ordinary places, times, and things of human work, we recognize that Christ comes to us in the Supper as gift, transforming our work, too, into a gift from the Creator. The Supper, in no small part, anticipates the consummation of the world in Jesus Christ, work in which we, too, have a part. As this bread is taken, blessed, broken, and given for us, our work is drawn into the life of the world. Yet the larger patterns of work in American society often contradict the gift of life in the work of Jesus Christ. For a fuller vision of human labor, therefore, one must attend to systemic issues of how work is distributed, how it is hoarded, and how a eucharistic economy works toward the transformation of workplace and economy for the worker. To those issues I turn in the final chapter.

5

Working for a Living

Work, the Economy, and the Common Good

God's life seeks and draws all creatures, granting them communion and life not because they have done good work, but out of the grace of divine excess. God does not withhold, but gives to the creature God's very self, so that all might have life abundantly. This gift, I have argued, can result in the humanization of work when we attend the divine rhythms. The God who works on our behalf creates a eucharistic people who respond by offering themselves in work given for others, however modest and incomplete those labors may be. For our labors to be responsive, however, wider circles of accountability must exist. It becomes difficult to envision humane work, in other words, in sweatshops that exploit children, in societies that value workers only insofar as they are producers and consumers, and in economies where efficiency alone reigns. God's work encompasses more than individual workers; that work lures communities as well. God's work does not simply order the household on a small scale, but beckons the economy at large. Most of the time, these larger collectives of human persons spurn God's work, just as individual workers do, resulting in systems of power that hoard wealth at the expense of others, own the work of wage slaves, and reduce persons to the work they produce. But God's work has something larger in mind: the luring of all creation into God's reign, where work will no longer produce weapons of war and slaves who know only work. That reign invites us to find a home in God's work and life, a home where slavery ends and swords are beaten into plowshares. A theological vision of work, then, must pay attention to the economy, the ways in which economies distribute work, and the ways we measure economic growth. For work to flourish, the larger household must also thrive.

The main focus of attention in this chapter is the U.S. economy and how it orders work. But the U.S. economy, obviously, does not exist in isolation. Indeed, in an age of multinational corporations, it becomes increasingly difficult to mark where the U.S. economy ends and that of other nations begins. The chapter, then, offers only a glance at selected facets of our increasingly global economy, and how some of the theological themes we have examined might inform a revitalization of work. My own economic expertise, as the reader will quickly discover, is inadequate for the task at hand. But my intent is neither to offer a definitive portrait of the U.S. economy nor to prescribe remedies for current ills within it that affect workers. Rather, my intent is to ask questions of the ways in which the U.S. economy orders and values workers' lives and to offer some general theological principles that might enhance the flourishing of all within that economy. Economics and Christian theology, after all, are both concerned with planetary flourishing, even if they begin from radically different perspectives (as economics begins with the person as consumer/producer and theology with God's grace to the world in Christ and the Spirit). Despite their different starting points, economics and Christian theology can learn from each other. The present chapter is simply one attempt to add to that conversation, to pose economic questions that are also theological ones, in the conviction that the flourishing of all creation is in the interest of both economics and Christian theology. Nonetheless, the general suggestions outlined here remain very much theological, with all the limitations and inadequacies that "theology" implies.

The U.S. economy is probably the most religiously pluralistic of all economies on the planet. This theological analysis of economic questions, therefore, does not argue that Christianity fills a conspicuous gap in the U.S. economy. Neither do I suggest that persons of other religious traditions must accept the theological claims herein to participate in the flourishing of the *oikos*. Both of these turns would be coercive, incommensurable with the God of grace whom Christians encounter in Jesus Christ. Christian theology, however, does offer a unique perspective on the way work and goods are distributed and shared. The theological claims that I magnify are important for economic life not because they must be accepted by all persons as doctrine in order for flourishing to occur, but because they offer a vision of the common good, where all creatures participate in abundant life. Much of what follows, undoubtedly, could be traced via other religious vocabularies and traditions. Abundant life is hardly the property of Christianity alone. But Christianity does offer unique strains in that life, strains that the broken household desperately needs to hear. Theological reflection enhances and agitates our vision of the economy: how work is shared or owned, how full employment might become reality, how Sabbath and rest are good for the work of the household, how growth includes more than consumption and production, how private property enhances the sharing of goods, and finally, how a Reformed vision of the *oikos* might invoke the Roman Catholic principle of subsidiarity and avoid the extremes of global capitalism and socialism that ultimately denigrate workers and good work.

OWNING WORK AND BEING OWNED BY OTHERS

Self-employment provides many American workers with a legitimate sense of ownership. Many writers, artists, physicians, small-business owners, consultants, and musicians make immediate decisions that affect their pace of work and how much they work, while they acknowledge the work of others. In order to be self-employed, in other words, one needs others' labor. In some respects, self-employment offers a glimpse at work that fosters interdependence and distinctive gifts, since such work does not belong to itself long. But most workers in the U.S. economy are not self-employed. Most of us work for someone else, and often encounter problems when the products of our labors are owned by others. Who owns the work of those of us who are not self-employed, but who work for larger businesses, the government, or a school system? Can good work be practiced in these contexts?

Economic history is replete with examples of work owned by someone other than the worker. On many reads, the edifice of civilization appears built on the backs of laborers who did not benefit much from their work. Whether they lugged bricks for the Great Wall, hoed fields in the Fertile Crescent, laid stone for Notre Dame, or terraced steps at Manchu Picchu, many who did the hardest work reaped little in return. These workers may have labored in exchange for a wage, or if they were slaves, in exchange for their lives. If workers did not perform as ordered, they were often subject to severe discipline by the overseer. Indeed, much of what constituted discipline was window dressing for owners and overseers who wielded power over workers. For slaves on the North American continent, where the power dynamics were most brutal, the slave, as the property of the master, could be disposed as the master saw fit: submitted to ceaseless labor, beaten, raped, degraded, burned, or lynched. Chattel slavery frames the beginning of the U.S. economy, a practice of owning other workers—and their work—as property.[1]

Though the abuses of such ownership have faded with Emancipation, many American workers still experience their work, and at times themselves, as owned by others. Wage labor provides its own form of ownership: one works for a company in exchange for money from company coffers. The products and ideas that one contributes to the company then become the property of the firm rather than the worker. In many instances, this approximates a fair exchange: workers supply a company with a necessary skill, a skill that enables them to live. One works *for a living*. Indeed, some level of interdependence manifests itself in these arrangements: companies cannot exist without skilled workers; skilled workers need wages to live; both needs are met as work is exchanged for wages. When workers say that they work "for IBM" or "for General Motors," they are telling the truth.

On the other hand, some forms of wage labor separate workers from the management and ownership of work and militate against the interdependence of managers and workers. When labor is seen over against management, and vice versa, a competitive scenario often unfolds: managers, in the name of efficiency and profit, try to squeeze the most work from workers, while workers resist managers as illegitimate owners of their labors. Conflict between labor and management, of course, has its own lengthy history, in no small part because workers often feel that they have little voice in the day-to-day operations of the company that affect their working conditions. The irony of many modern management/worker models is that those closest to the labor routines, those who know the work best—on the assembly line or the shop floor, or at the laboratory apparatus—are often most distanced from the decisions that affect their labor. Work, in this sense, is neither shared nor viewed as interdependent, but as a commodity that one controls via other workers.

Such constructions of work obviously run counter to the theological themes I have explored throughout this book. Furthermore, such constructions that stress ownership, control, and competition ultimately drain work of its life; the only economy that is life-sustaining is an economy that shares work and recognizes workers' interdependence. As the divine life nourishes the world in the distinctive work of Father, Son, and Holy Spirit, no one person owns the work of another. The triune life is what gives us life, underscoring the essential need for sharing and interdependence in our own lives. When work is hoarded or owned exclusively by another, workers experience either the withering death of alienation from their labors or brutal death at the hands of the master. An economy that responds to the divine life, by contrast, does everything it can to spread ownership of work across all workers, to move away from conflictual strategies in the workplace, and to avoid the dehumanization of hyper-specialized work.

Cornel West, following Marx, has claimed that capitalism invariably alienates workers from their work: "Capitalism is an antidemocratic mode of socioeconomic organization in that it requires the removal of control of production from those engaged in production."[2] In order for the accumulation of capital to profit, the owners of capital must extract as much labor as possible from their workers without fully attending workers' voices. Left to itself, the machinery of the market leans toward increasingly hierarchical forms of power, where those closest to the hard, manual labor have the least voice in its employment. The extreme example, of course, is slavery, which appears in the U.S. context at its national beginnings. Cotton trade, the linchpin of the southern economy that fed a hungry industrial North, was built with the blood of chattel slaves.[3] Efficiency and profit alone do not guarantee that work is shared or that the products of good work are distributed equitably. Indeed, left to its own devices, the market often steers in the direction of inequality. Even hard-line capitalists agree there has rarely been a "free" market. Occasional interventions—or major structural changes, such as the abolition of slavery—are needed to create the conditions for better work, more democratic systems of organization, and more equitable distribution of resources among workers.[4]

Even if one argues with West's proposal for a recovery of the progressive Marxist tradition to aid Christians in the construction of a livable future, his critique is relevant for a theology of work. Any system that fosters the domination of others through work is suspect on theological grounds. Though work cannot make us free, when work is a response to the divine life, it can be an expression of freedom and creativity. Work that responds in this manner seeks collaboration rather than conflict, sharing rather than ownership alone. On these measurements, the current distribution of labor along capitalist lines comes up rather short.

What, then, might be some alternative systemic arrangements that expand the practice of good work explored in this book? One start would be to expand worker/employee ownership of firms and amplify worker voices in management decisions. A Christian understanding of work emphasizes the intrinsic value of the worker first and foremost. Valuing the worker—above profit, above efficiency—is essential not merely because without workers no work is being done (the utilitarian value of workers), but because each worker is uniquely and irreplaceably created in God's image. The value of workers reflects not merely the work they do, but is grounded in the persons they are and whose they are, God's. Because good work is shared, because it recognizes interdependence on other forms of work, prevalent modes of corporate governance are suspect. Corporate practices that separate shop-floor workers from management, which give employees little stake in the ownership of the firm, effectively mean that workers' labor is owned by others. Such arrangements, as one surveys the course of labor history in the United States, often erupt in protracted labor/management feuds. When workers have a stake in the profitability of a corporation beyond their paychecks, however, management and labor recognize their own work as interdependent. Those closest to the actual manufacture of goods—the people who assemble computer chips, fasten doors to cars, and bind books—have a voice in how that labor is configured. Fostering arrangements of employee ownership and governance not only echoes the theological claims we have explored, such an approach makes good business sense. Employee satisfaction tends to grow, productivity increases, and workers tend to stay with firms longer (meaning there is less need and expense for continual training of new workers) when workers experience a firm's increased investment in them and as they invest their gifts in that workplace. It is in the interest of both management and labor for these kinds of ownership arrangements to flourish.

These forms of ownership do not mean that distinctions between management and labor disappear. As we have already explored, there is intrinsic value to *distinctive* work. When God labors on behalf of creation, the different gifts of workers are honored and incorporated into the divine life. Promoting all workers to management status neither honors distinctive work nor utilizes unique gifts to their fullest potential. The key to good work is not the abolition of workplace distinctions, but whether management, labor, and stockholders understand their labors as interrelated and shared or conflicted and hoarded. When work is shared, those whose labors are closest to the actual production of goods and services have significant voice in the governance of the workplace.

Several attempts at collaborative governance in the workplace have emerged in the last several decades on the American scene; they have been in place even longer in Europe and Japan. One of the more heralded experiments in this vein is the Saturn auto plant in Spring Hill, Tennessee. Offering an innovative model of assembly-line workers formed in teams that have significant voice in basic management decisions, offering workers vested stockholder interest in the corporation, Saturn has avoided many of the protracted battles between labor and management characteristic of other industrial firms. In many instances, the model seems to work, as employee morale is high, the company is profitable, and the cars rank highly in quality and performance. Good work emerges from the Saturn plant. Yet the model has its skeptics, and upon closer examination, not all of the conditions of a collaborative workplace seem to be in place. Attempts to organize a branch of the United Auto Workers were consistently rebuffed by management and viewed as a threat to good work. Many plant workers express skepticism about whether management really values their input in larger decisions. Teamwork, moreover, could at times stifle creativity and isolate workers who did not fit the company mold.[5]

Attempts at the democratization of the workplace, in other words, can be co-opted by the search for profitability. The team can smother individual voices within it; managers can listen to employees cynically while promoting their own interests all the while. Yet the Saturn experiment represents a step, even if it is not yet fully implemented, toward an increased integration of the shared labors that constitute good work. A society that sought to continue such work would encourage a proliferation of these steps.

One of the realities that has prevented the Saturn model from being fully implemented is the persistence of labor/management conflict, perhaps in submerged forms. The tendency throughout American economic life has been to construe labor and management as having two distinct and often competing interests. Workers want a decent wage; management wants increasing profitability to balloon company coffers. The former will increasingly demand the most they can get without putting the firm out of business, while the latter will extract as much as possible from workers for as little as possible. A zero-sum game characterizes much of this history, where gains in a firm's profitability are at the expense of worker compensation and vice versa. Yet an alternative assumption is possible, one that is quite plausible given our theological exploration: abundance and sharing rather than competing, conflicting interests. The dynamic of divine life shows us that when good work is shared, its bounty increases, filling the creature with God's goodness. If workers and management recognized that the good of their work increased through sharing and collaboration, then perhaps corporate governance would see unionization less as a threat and more as a voice for the continued flourishing of work, the products of good work, and the profits that stem from good work. The interest of both management and labor, after all, is the creation of good products and services; the maintenance of a decent standard of living that comes, in part, from good labor; and the continued ecological sustainability of work practices. When the labors that enable these interests to become reality are shared, one catches a glimpse of good work in action.

Another systemic shift that promotes good work is to reject the hyperspecialization of workers that typically results from corporate models that prize efficiency above all else. The high point of this movement was the "scientific management" school of F. W. Taylor. Taylor believed that the more one could subdivide the intricate processes of assembly-line work into discrete, simple tasks, the more one removed "brain work" from the shop floor, the more widgets a factory could produce and the greater control management would have over workplace efficiency and profitability.[6] Such methods held sway for several decades after the introduction of assembly-line work, resulting in deadening and monotonous toil that crippled the worker. Herman Daly and John Cobb note the inconsistencies in valuing efficiency over worker creativity: "The profoundly dehumanizing character of so much work is a function of the inherent drive of the system toward productivity through specialization. There seems to be an inherent tension between humanly satisfying work and the quantity of production per worker."[7] Taylorism places efficiency (one of the results of work) over the worker and hence violates the principle of valuing workers for who they are and whose they are. One sees in Taylorism an example of drives toward one aim of work run amok: intolerable working conditions are adopted and justified so long as efficiency increases. Any system that values ends over people is idolatrous, and though Taylorism has declined since its heyday, its grandchildren are present in more disguised forms. Efficiency continues as a bottom line for innumerable firms, and in the name of it pension plans are slashed or eliminated (as in the case of United Airlines in 2005), persons are disposable targets for downsizing, and workers in large firms become increasingly specialized so that their distinctive work is often removed from each other. A society that values workers more than their work, that refuses to reduce people to the goods they produce, will encourage both worker ownership of firms as well as a move away from hyper-specialization within those firms. When firms instruct workers in one task, those workers are unemployable once that task becomes obsolete. When, by contrast, workers are introduced to some breadth of work that is shared, the abundance of work continues long after particular tasks have faded. Employment then becomes not a privilege, but a way in which society draws on the gifts of all workers.

EMPLOYMENT: SCARCITY OR ABUNDANCE?

In the first chapter I surveyed some patterns of employment, unemployment, and underemployment in the U.S. economy. As I write these pages, we are experiencing an acceptable level of unemployment slightly more than 5 percent. Bearing in mind that this statistic does not include the long-term unemployed and those who have given up the search for work altogether, the actual number of unemployed is at least one percentage point higher. How, we should ask, did it become acceptable for close to one in ten workers to be without paid work? Unemployment is a confounding problem in the United States, not merely for the workers who are no longer able to pay rent and buy clothes for their children, but for the well-being of society at large. A society that tolerates this number of unemployed tolerates a waste of working resources and assumes that some will be unable to practice their gifts in the workplace. A society such as this has inured itself to something less than abundant life. In clear opposition to the work of divine abundance, this society assumes that jobs are scarce, and that some will have them and others will not.

How different the strains of Christian theology ring. The divine life, the work of the divine persons, is not about competition for scarce resources, but about the sharing of superfluous abundance. Kathryn Tanner writes perceptively of this alternative economic view:

> What is notable about Christianity as a field, what is unusual about it, is its attempt to institute a circulation of goods to be possessed by all in the same fullness of degree without diminution or loss, a distribution that in its prodigal promiscuity calls forth neither the pride of superior position nor rivalrous envy among its recipients. . . . The good is distributed by God and is to be distributed by us in imitation of God, in an indiscriminate, profligate fashion that fails to reflect the differences in worthiness and status that rule the arrangements of a sinful world. The purpose of the giving is elevation, without limit, so as to bring all recipients to the level of the giver, ultimately God.[8]

The eucharistic banquet, we have seen, is a response of God's people to the kind of giving that God initiates. Bringing ourselves and tokens of our work in the bread and wine, we receive God's very self in the breaking and sharing of that food and drink. God gives, we give, and God keeps on giving: the economy of the table is inexhaustible. Here one does not compete for scarce resources or a finite number of blessings. Rather, here at table that blessing is given for all, regardless of status or work. In God's superfluous giving, we are made partakers in God's very life. In that life, abundance is shared.

Is it possible to organize a society along the assumption that work can be shared in abundance rather than subject to competition and scarcity? Certainly there is enough work to be done, more than enough until time runs its course. One step in moving from scarcity to abundance would be to recognize work as a fundamental right of the human person, one aspect of what it means to be a child of God. The U.S. Catholic bishops' letter on the economy contains this assumption: "Employment is a basic right, a right which protects the freedom of all to participate in the economic life of society."[9] Note how the bishops couch this language of rights not as something to be held for oneself, as a libertarian construal of rights, but as right to participate in community. I do not clamor for work because it is scarce, and demand it as my right alone; work, rather, is one of the ways in which persons bind themselves to one another in society. Work, in an echo of the divine life, is an expression of communion, to which all God's creatures have the right of access. Robust societies do not tolerate systems where many are permanently without work and lack full access to that society's life, but seek policies of full employment.

What, practically speaking, would such policies resemble? One recent attempt in American domestic policy was the Clinton administration's institution of welfare reform or "workfare," which sought to tie government entitlements to meaningful work. To receive government aid, one had to be involved in work conducive to the good of society. This linkage of assistance to work, proponents claimed, offered incentives to meaningful work and the promise of a more productive nation. One often unacknowledged consequence of these policies, of course, was a drastic reduction in government assistance for those *not* working. Though such policies might be applauded for their attempt to employ the gifts of the chronically unemployed in meaningful occupations, they also operate out of the assumption that there are two classes of persons on government assistance: the "deserving" and "undeserving" poor. Such assumptions are problematic as a response to God's abundant giving, which indiscriminately bestows on all, regardless of an individual's worthiness. Tanner writes, "Humans should try to distribute the gift of God as God does, without concern for whether they are deserved by their recipients."[10] If work is to be shared, if the abundance of creation is to be given to all, then the distribution of work and abundance cannot proceed along workfare lines.

An alternative policy would be to dismantle the connection between government assistance and employment by providing training and education for all who are unemployed. Here, there would be no means testing of recipients. Rather, local, state, and federal governments could offer several measures that enhance the participation of all in the reality of abundance, such as free education, job training, child care, and transportation. Enhanced educational options for the unemployed would satisfy both a society's need for an educated workforce and the unemployed person's desire to contribute in some way to life abundant. Apprenticeship programs for the unemployed would allow for the continuation of struggling trades (such as Navajo rug-weaving) and the creation of abundant beauty for society as a whole. The key, however, is not simply to construe public assistance as grants of money, but to include education, job training, and transportation to work as means of government assistance.[11]

Instead of linking welfare to work, governments—as one of the guardians of the public good—would seek to make access to economic participation in society broad for everyone. Full employment—drawing on the gifts of all people in meaningful work—would still be a goal of public policy, but a job would not be the means test to public assistance. Rather, echoing Tanner, the only test would be need. Jobs alone are not the panacea for a society that limits the participation of many in economic life. More important than a short-term job are the apprenticeship and education necessary for employment in trades, professions, and skilled labors. It is in everyone's interest to participate in a society with an educated workforce, as the skills that are gained in education invariably redound to better, more skilled labors. The money invested in free educational and training programs would pay for itself many times over as it represents an investment in people who do good work and pass on that gift to others.

But what of those persons who do not find employment after participating in educational programs and job training? In such cases, the government could serve as the employer of last resort, drawing on the skilled labors of the unemployed by providing a wage slightly below private-sector norms, so as to main-

tain incentives to find work outside government programs. Such jobs would
be offered to all according to need, not the worthiness of the worker. Large-
scale examples of analogous programs were present during the Great Depres-
sion, such as the Civilian Conservation Corps and Works Progress
Administration. The enduring legacy and accomplishments of these programs
continue long after their demise and include national treasures such as the
Golden Gate Bridge and Timberline Lodge on Mount Hood, Oregon. Children of all ages in countless cities cool off on summer days in swimming pools
and parks that date from this era. The creation of these facilities, which drew
on the ranks of the unemployed, are impossible to price, since they represent
public goods that are accessible to all. Such facilities bring environmental
gems within reach for much of the nation and cultivate the aesthetic values and
quality of life of the nation at large. Keeping this history in mind, a short-term
job offered by the government might redound easily to long-term public good.
Job programs need not be as large or extensive as the CCC or WPA; they need
only draw on the skills of persons previously unemployed and address a wider
public need. Full employment, in this model, is not simply placing every person in a job provided by the state, but ensuring that structures are in place to
enable the economic participation of all members of society. Work is one
means of participation in that society, and it is also the way that most of us gain
a livelihood. A society that makes a commitment to full employment recognizes that the well-being of a society is bound up with the flourishing of its
people's gifts, especially gifts that are yet to be discovered.

REST IN AN OVERWORKED SOCIETY

Good work recognizes the need for rest. As we have seen in this study, work
is not the measure of human being; rather, the measure of our lives is reflected
in belonging to God, communion with God, and our response to God. Whatever work we do (or do not do), we already live from God. The Bible portrays
God at work and God at rest, rhythms that are built into the fabric of creation.
None of God's creatures, except human beings, work their fingers to the bone.
Fields lie fallow; birds and bees rest; bears hibernate; oak trees shed their
leaves in the fall. We alone choose to ignore the Sabbath. One of the pathologies of American work habits is that we often think we cannot work enough.
Incentives to stay on the job abound, from the elusive promotion to overtime
pay to the accolades of our peers. Americans seem to be working longer (and
harder) than ever, even when millions of us are looking for work. In the 1960s,
futurists painted a world where leisure would increase and our time on the job
would decline rapidly. That world has evaporated as the Mists of Avalon,

replaced with a world where work has become home and home has become work. For many of us, work now has become synonymous with identity: I "am" a teacher, an engineer, a truck driver, and we log enough hours per day on the job to justify that identity. This odd dynamic, moreover, appears contradictory: the more we work, the less we can envision ourselves not working. In many cases, the imposition of longer hours on the job actually leads to addiction: I work, therefore I am. And if such is the case, we will not be able to work enough.

Clearly, these work habits fly in the face of the way God works and the way God summons us to respond to that Great Work. At the beginning of the Christian workweek is the Sabbath, the reminder that God both hallows our lives and our work, summoning us to rest from our labors. Is it conceivable that the rhythms of our national patterns of work might resonate with the movements of work and rest we encounter in the biblical Sabbath?

One step would be to recover patterns of rest in American consumption patterns. It is now possible in nearly every town larger than five thousand people to shop for groceries at any hour of the day, devour a cheeseburger at 2 a.m., and catch a midnight movie. We can now consume at all hours, nonstop to our belly's delight. Factories, meanwhile, churn out products without ceasing, humming their engines through the night. While these conveniences tend to make life exciting, they do come at a cost: low-wage and sleep-deprived workers must staff the stores and restaurants where we get our fill in the middle of the night. Children of these workers are left home alone or in hasty care arrangements. The result for consumers, moreover, has not been an improvement of living standard. Amid the million pounds of snack foods and countless video rentals, we are not any happier. Instead, we're overweight, overstimulated, and exhausted.

One response might be to reinstitutionalize blue laws in municipalities, yet such a response is a desperate attempt to reclaim rest, instituting it from above in a feeble mimicking of the Sabbath command. A more helpful first step, rather, would be to curb our highly consumptive habits. Until Americans realize that the richness of life is not measured in things, we will work and devour without ceasing. More helpful in this regard are the multiple movements at the core of religious traditions to recover simplicity: a simplicity rediscovered in relationship with the earth, other people, and the Creator.[12] We can learn to live with fewer things that we buy only at limited hours of the day; 8 a.m. to 7 p.m. should suffice. This recognition, however, can only be achieved by a kind of conversion that is not possible by imposing blue laws—that is, recognizing that a life well-lived is a life shared with others. Rest will happen if people can rest in the simplicity that we are made for God and each other.

One item of governmental legislation that would be well-served, however, is the creation of laws that mandate paid vacation time. Currently, in the United States, no federal law requires employers to offer employees even a week of vacation. This lack means that if one's employer were to suddenly implement a policy of no vacation time, the employee would have no recourse to protest or request a vacation. On this score, we are an oddity, not merely in the "developed" world, but also among our "developing" neighbors. Brazil mandates twenty-four to thirty days of paid vacation annually; China requires fifteen days of paid leave each year.[13] Our conspicuous lack of vacation simply mirrors our insatiable practice of more and more work. Perhaps it should not surprise the nation that even those who have vacation time often do not take advantage of it. A society that believes that identity comes through work, that one cannot ever work hard enough, will not take time off. Legislation that stipulated minimal vacation time, however, would be rather easy to implement, and could even be accomplished without declines in economic productivity. Nearly every European nation has generous vacation policies in comparison to us, and many, such as Norway, Belgium, the Netherlands, and Italy, consistently outstrip the United States in worker productivity.[14] Are these productivity rates, perhaps, the result of a better-rested workforce? A society that considers vacation a universal entitlement recognizes that the value of human persons is not found only in the things they produce. By valuing rest, such societies place a premium on *people*, and good work abounds as a result.

Even if the national government was reluctant to implement legislative measures, the practice of paid vacation could easily become institutionalized in corporate culture simply by shutting down, or drastically curtailing normal operations for a week or two per year. Such patterns are already in place in many national institutions, including education and government, and are the norm in the private sector in nations such as Italy and Spain. These slowdowns in the work year may in fact lead to a rise in worker productivity, especially as compared with the United States.[15] Good work is done when it is incorporated into patterns of rest; when rest disappears, workers not only become blind to the patterns of the divine work, they soon become trapped in work that is addictive drudgery. To work well is to know that we are not made for work alone.

MEASURING ECONOMIC GROWTH:
CONSUMPTION OR COMMUNITY?

One of the national myths that feeds our workplace patterns is our unwavering commitment to economic growth, the idea that the economy can expand indefinitely amid the competition for scarce resources on a global scale. The rising tide, we are promised, will lift all boats, or at least the boats that ride the current of the New World Order. We work, in no small part, to ensure continued economic growth, both to the fattening of our wallets and the boon of the nation's wealth. In work, we compete for scarce resources and consume those that we can find. Workers of the past century were held captive to this myth, and American history has borne out its supposed truth. Our standard of living has increased dramatically over the past one hundred years, so long as we ignore the poor (whose numbers have swelled over the past thirty years). Consumer conveniences that were once out of reach for the middle class are now commonplace; so, too, is a house of one's own. Growth, we are told, has made this good life accessible. Indeed, it is nearly impossible to imagine a candidate for public office campaigning on any economic platform other than growth and consumption. Imagine the absurdity of a politician claiming that we needed to consume and live with less! The dominant paradigm in our construction of growth has been to tie growth to consumption: a society that grows economically is a society that uses up more things and services. Occasionally, this growth meets a downturn (hence, the American bust at the dawn of the new millennium), but overall, societies that increase consumption are the beneficiaries of a steadily increasing boom.

The contrast with the theological principles we have explored in this book are not immediately evident here. The dynamics of divine giving, too, seek to increase abundance among all God's people. Both consumptive growth and divine giving, it seems, are concerned with the well-being, flourishing, and distribution of goods. But a crucial difference emerges upon closer examination: where economic mythology weds growth to consumption, the work of the divine economy ties growth to giving. God gives and works out of abundance (*pleroma*), not scarcity. As God gives to creation, creation returns to God. The giving increases resources rather than limiting them; as God gives, creatures are enabled to give in return, contributing themselves and receiving even more in return, not because their response is good, but because God's gift keeps on giving. The problem with current reigning measurements of growth, then, is that they are fixed too firmly to consumption, the using up of resources and gifts. As a result, work and gifts that cannot be consumed fall by the wayside—the unpaid work that sustains health, friendship, the pursuit of knowledge, family, and the daily tasks of homemaking. A society that cared about abundance and growth would draw this immeasurable work into its account of economic life.

John Cobb has dubbed this paradigm of growth "economism"—"the belief that society should be organized for the sake of economic growth. Those who hold this belief assume that economic growth is good for human beings."[16] Economism has the ring of a truism: of course, growth is good! But has economic growth led to the flourishing of human community? Glancing at the past thirty years of American life, it is not evident that growth has been only the bearer of good news. The phenomenal expansion of the U.S. economy since the end of World War II, especially in the past few decades, has not resulted in increased prosperity for all; in fact, it seems to have accelerated rates of poverty. Growth, moreover, has not led to an increase in meaningful work. Cobb and Daly point to the surges in part-time work and rates of unemployment that have accompanied the rise in national GDP.[17] A national study cites the anomaly of job stagnation in a time of economic growth.[18] Growth and prosperity translate all too often into doldrums of unemployment for many skilled workers, not the days of leisure promised decades ago.

Compounding this lack of sharing in abundance and prosperity in times of economic growth are the disturbing environmental implications of current measurements. What matters in measurements of economic growth is the flow and creation of money and wealth, the consumption of resources rather than their conservation. Sallie McFague notes that "the GDP counts 'harmful' activities the same as 'beneficial' ones, the clear-cutting of an old-growth forest as well as crime and social decay—whatever brings money into the pockets of some individuals counts."[19] The mythology of growth now counts pollution as a positive good, so long as someone can profit from its production, clean-up, and maintenance. Clearly these measurements alone are not the gauge of a healthy, working society. The problem, in brief, is that they measure only what can be used up, rather than what can be sustained and nurtured to keep on giving. In using up the resources of a finite planet, however, we make the rooms of the household less and less inhabitable.

If current measurements of economic growth fail to take into account ecological sustainability and fall prey to the vision that endless acquisition is a public good, the true measurements of the good life are notoriously difficult to measure. Practices of abundance exist in the midst of growth economies, but they often occur at the fringes of consumer society. In an aptly titled volume, *The Good Life*, David Matzko McCarthy notes the superfluity of these fringe labors:

> People teach night courses for pittance; they garden for enjoyment and give away tomatoes. Some parents coach soccer for free. In a consumer economy, it is often outside the dominant market where the real production is at work, where we get off the treadmill and put our efforts and skill to cultivating common life and doing good work. . . . There is an interesting excess and uselessness to the kind of work that is directed toward the goods of human life.[20]

What sustains the good of society, in other words, is not the endless growth of purchasing power, but the relationships made possible in the good work of

the community. Many of these labors—from parenting to gardening to tutor-
ing to singing in the church choir—cannot be measured by reigning economic
indices. Neither should they be reduced to their economic benefit; relationships simply cannot be quantified. But it is conceivable that measurements of
economic health could factor in these wider, "ancillary" concerns. One of
these alternative measures is the United Nations Human Development Index
(HDI), which includes life expectancy and educational levels in addition to traditional gauges of economic growth.[21] Education and life expectancy, though
they do not quantify relationships, do point to wider networks of health care
and schooling that are essential for relationships to flourish. Though other
qualities of abundant societies will never be measured—the patience of parenting, the devotion of marriages, the giving of friendships—there are ways of
accounting for health that do not reduce persons to the products they produce
or the money they earn. When abundance is shared, money is not the only
matter. Good work, after all, concerns the whole person, and the common
good of society.

   These considerations should lead us to reject growth for growth's sake. As
Douglas Meeks puts it, "Growth should not be based on infinite needs and
acquisition leading to an ever-widening appropriation of nature for the sake
of accumulation of wealth as power. Rather growth should be a deepening of
human capacities for the service of human development within community."[22]
God's economy of abundance recognizes that consumption will never satisfy.
In an odd and seemingly quixotic counterpoint to a society of gain, the divine
economy claims that abundance is enjoyed in giving it away: the giving of oneself in friendship, parenting, and marriage, the giving of society's resources so
that all are educated and have adequate health care, the giving of land to others so that it may be enjoyed by all.

   In our work and in our rest we are always more than economic creatures.
Our jobs, the GDP, and personal income do not define who we are. We are
who we are because we belong to God and are drawn in the divine life toward
others. As McCarthy writes, "In an economy directed to the good of human
life, our assets are found in the cultivation of arts, in sacrifice for the sake of
beauty and truth, in dance, games of strategy and wit, in housing construction
and other constructive labors, and in businesses that make and provide what
is good for common life—not only tables and chairs, but also baseball fields,
hot dogs, and cold drinks."[23] To claim that the health of a society is bound up
in growth alone is to submit to an idol. The good work that sustains community, perhaps, can never be measured economically, because that work is typically unpaid. But these unpaid labors mirror the divine economy most closely
and foster the common good of society most effectively. Composing songs that
will never be released on CD, coaching children who will never make the big

leagues, loving a spouse in his nakedness and vulnerability are all economically useless, perhaps even silly and superfluous. But they are all gifts that magnify giving and abundance beyond any one person's attempt to comprehend. Our accounts of flourishing societies, too, ought to recognize as much.

PRIVATE PROPERTY AND COMMON GOOD

Property has been highly contestable throughout the history of the Christian church. The earliest Christians struggled against the notion that property was the exclusive domain of those who owned it: "All who believed were together and had all things in common; they would sell their possessions and goods and distribute the proceeds to all, as any had need" (Acts 2:44–45). Property, for these Christians, was given away so that others could benefit. Capitalism, by contrast, has tended to dangle private property as one of the promises of a good society: as incentive for hard work, as encouragement for accumulation in the name of continued prosperity. And, in a secular retort to early church practices, some schools of socialism seek to replace private property with societal collectivism, where the goods of a society are owned by the state, and hence all people. What is the relation of property to work? I would suggest that private property serves the common good not in the way that capitalism envisions, but in the sense that it connects good work to the land, however tenuously, and insofar as it enables one to give property away. This strange dynamic is at the heart of the Acts narrative: in having, one gives. Good work does not entail the abolition of private property, but its continued flourishing as it is given away and received.

In *Rerum Novarum*, Leo XIII makes a connection that is often forgotten in the postindustrial world: "All human subsistence is derived either from labor on one's own land, or from some toil, some calling, which is paid for either in the produce of the land itself, or in that which is exchanged for what the land brings forth."[24] Work is always related to land, made possible because of the resources of the land, and enables us to live from the bounty the land produces. No labor occurs apart from or removed from the land. Computer programming draws on minerals mined from the earth's crust; legal systems are attempts to live civilly on the land with one another; teaching entails the instruction of students in the beauty and bounty of the land; proclaiming the gospel draws on bread and wine harvested from fields of the earth; and all of these kinds of work are exchanged for food and resources reaped from the land. Good work draws us toward the land, reminds us of our indelible connection to earth, and teaches us to tread lightly. Destructive work pretends that we do not live from the earth and encourages roughshod ranging.

Access to land is also a prerequisite to good work. During the Reconstruc-
tion era in the American South, the phrase "forty acres and a mule" was a slogan of emancipated slaves. The idea was simple: if the recently liberated had
access to some land and a beast to help cultivate it, good work could be done
for oneself and one's community. A little land would make possible not mere
subsistence farming so that one's family could be fed, but the creation of good
work for generations to come. On the plantation slaves knew well the horror
of working on others' land, for others' benefit alone. Denying slaves access to
land during slavery was a means of disempowerment and subjugation; continued denial of access to land ensured the continuation of oppression—and the
perpetuation of bad work in tenant farming—long after slavery had been abol-
ished. The cry for forty acres and a mule was not simply a claim to what one
deserved; it was a recognition that the common good is served when all have
access to land that yields decent work.

In his encyclical written a few decades after Emancipation, Leo echoes this
claim: "The law, therefore, should favor ownership, and its policy should be
to induce as many as possible of the people to become owners."[25] The reasons
for encouraging ownership are diverse: it lessens the gap between rich and
poor, it promotes a legitimate sense of pride in one's labors,[26] and a sense of
fellowship and common bond with one's neighbors in the land. As creatures
of the earth, *adamah*, each person and her/his work can be grounded in a plot
of land. Obviously, the ideal of forty acres and a mule is neither practical nor
attainable in the tightly packed metropolises where an increasing majority of
U.S. citizens live. But the principle of being grounded in a place of one's own
is still germane: ownership of one's dwelling, too, is a form of connection to
land, home, and community where good work can emerge. That is why policies such as low-interest HUD mortgages make good public policy and should
be increased, and also why programs such as Habitat for Humanity have
achieved remarkable successes. When persons have a place to call their own,
abundance continues.

The point of private property, however, is not simply to hold on to what
one has. If possession is the goal of connecting labor to land, then the economy of scarcity reigns supreme once again. In the United States, hoarding private property has become commonplace: those with the means increasingly
find refuge in secluded gated communities, flee to vacation homes in remote
locations (or on private islands), and buy up more land precisely so they can
enjoy it by themselves. Like any other desire, the appetite for a place of one's
own can become insatiable. The divine economy, however, reminds us that
one has in order to give away. The scandal of the early Christians was not that
they gave up their private property to a larger collective; countless experiments in human history have attempted as much. Rather, the scandal was that

they subverted an economy of scarcity, recognizing that abundance flourished and increased when these followers of the Way invited others to share in their possessions.

Interpreters often attribute this holding of things in common to asceticism or a willingness to let go of what one holds dear. Typically, we read Acts 2 and begrudgingly admit that we, too, should live as the early Christians did, by surrendering more of what we have. But such interpretations obscure the abundance, joy, and excess of that early Christian community—a group that spent a lot of time eating, breaking bread "with glad and generous hearts" (v. 46), and rejoicing in the temple. These Christians enjoyed a lot of time together doing economically useless, but communally sustaining things, and they did so not out of begrudging denial, but gracious excess. When things were shared, there was more than enough for everyone. These practices are not begrudging asceticism, but an invitation into an abundant—and even riotous—life, where giving is inexhaustible.

Giving what one has does not mean that the reservoir of goods slowly runs dry; rather, one has to give, and in giving one has even more. We can glimpse this cycle in striking acts of public benevolence, as when a cattle rancher bequeaths land in the Davis Mountains of West Texas as a nature preserve, thus protecting native flora and allowing countless future generations, including the descendants of the cattle rancher, to walk this land for rejuvenation and the quiet contemplation that comes in the grandeur of a mountain range. But we glimpse this dynamic of having through giving not only there; we catch it in the tomatoes given from one's backyard garden, in the meals offered to others in the warmth of a kitchen, in conversation that attends to others' joy and sadness in the midst of an otherwise hectic day. Giving out of and from one's space, one's property, opens us to the gift of others. We have what is private in order to give away to others in work and thus have more.

SYSTEMS OF GOOD WORK IN A GLOBAL ECONOMY

Good work flourishes in contexts that value workers as persons, honor gifts and rest, and encourage having through giving. What are the larger economic systems that promote this kind of work? How does global capitalism match up to the theological vision outlined in this study? How might it compare to alternatives, such as a return to smaller, local-scale economies? The intention of this final section is not to offer a blueprint for a Christian understanding of the global economy, but to pose a few questions about how work, self-interest, the common good, and the dignity of workers are addressed in competing accounts and how they might be informed by greater covenantal emphases. Two theological principles that I have already examined are especially important: (1) the inherent and irreplaceable dignity of workers, created in God's image, and (2) understanding our work as a response to the work God has already done. The first principle prohibits us from endorsing any system that places the value of work above the worker; the second enables us to embrace good work while it prevents us from attributing inordinate value to our labors alone.

Global capitalism, in many circles of Christianity, has become a theological straw man, the mark of all obstructions to God's Reign, the chief instance of idolatry in creation. Diatribes against global capitalism are not difficult to find, and span the theological spectrum from evangelical to revisionist Christianity.[27] Indeed, the cutthroat forms of capitalism celebrated by reality TV programs such as *The Apprentice* are inimical to the theology I have emphasized throughout this study. Reality TV simply exaggerates what is already common in daily work. At its most basic level, capitalism assumes a scarcity of goods and resources, and argues that some form of self-interest is most conducive to the common good. Indeed, capitalism makes the same diagnosis of the human condition that Reformed Christianity does: human persons are in a desperate lot, mired in self-interest. But whereas Calvin understood self-interest as the fundamental obstacle to the good life, capitalism heralds it as a means to abundance. As Cobb and Daly put it, "Economic theory differed from Calvinism only in celebrating as rational what Calvinists confessed as sinful."[28] Because people crave for themselves, the key to satisfying these cravings is to direct them to the accumulation of capital, whose private growth will invariably redound to the common good. Accumulation, as its own good, produces more for all.

Obviously, this portrait is a gross oversimplification of capitalism, but its main brushstrokes would be accepted by most of its proponents. These emphases, however, should strike Christians as strange for several reasons. First, the vision of abundance is always couched in language of scarcity: there is never enough to be shared fully, so one must take what one can get in the hopes that what one has might redound to others' benefit. This language of scarcity is enormously problematic from a Christian perspective, where there is always room for one more at God's banqueting table. Second, capitalism clearly has not produced the benefits (at least in the past thirty years in the United States) that it purports to offer. The goods of accumulation, by contrast, have been hoarded, with wealth disparity now reaching levels only seen in the nation during the robber-baron era of the 1920s.[29] Assumptions of scarcity and accumulation alone do not allow for goods and gifts to be shared. Finally, self-interest alone, without an accompanying language of gift, results in a truncated vision of abundant life. The good life, we have seen, does not stem from having alone, but in giving away what one has. These observations suggest that unrestrained capitalism violates some of the fundamental emphases of a Christian perspective on the economy: the irreplaceable dignity of the worker in God's image and the drive to share in the abundance of creation. At the very least Christians need to ask whether present configurations of global capitalism emphasize accumulation, efficiency, and scarcity at the expense of workers and sharing. If they do, these present configurations are theologically bankrupt.

Socialism, or progressive Marxism, strikes many as an alternative to the abuses of capitalism. In varied forms, it has been embraced by some liberation theologians in Latin America, as well as public intellectuals such as Cornel West in the United States. In some respects the diagnosis of the human condition here is the same as in capitalism: the human person is insatiably bound to self-interest that can run amok and destroy itself. The key, contrary to capitalism, is to restrain inordinate self-interest by locating ownership of property, capital, and resources in larger collectives. These serve the commonweal by distributing the goods of society fairly and to all. Yet socialism of this form replicates assumptions of scarcity found in capitalism: because goods are scarce, the public needs to be protected from greedy capitalists that hoard. These assumptions are problematic, as we have already seen, since they smother abundance with an overriding attitude of scarcity. Practices of rationing that were commonplace in Eastern bloc nations only serve to confirm these attitudes. One easily gets the sense that a perfect socialist world would be one where what little there was to share was parceled out fairly, quite a different vision from the one we encounter in Acts 2.

On the issue of work, however, socialism is more intriguing. According to Marx, work is the chief means by which human persons create themselves. This assumption agrees with Christian theology insofar as it claims that because one works to create oneself, that work cannot be owned by others; rather, work provides a means of self-expression while it serves the larger community. But the fundamental assumption of Marxism is strikingly different from orthodox Christian theology: in work *we* create ourselves. This claim runs counter to the main theme of this book: in work we *respond* to the One who creates us. The danger, as I see it, in Marxist attitudes toward work is that they invariably replace faith in God with faith in one's work. (Though of course, for Marx, this is not a problem!) When work becomes our chief aim, moreover, we can readily and willingly trample over those who stand in the way of our supposedly good labors. Unwittingly, perhaps, Marxism risks valuing work over persons who do the work.

In response to the often-feuding visions of capitalism versus socialism, John Cobb and other progressive Christians have argued for a return to older, more primitive models of economic life. Echoing the environmentalist slogan "Think globally, act locally," Cobb suggests that we return to more locally inscribed economies, while acknowledging that they exist in an increasingly interconnected world. Local markets, the production of handicrafts in cottage industries, sustainable agricultural practices, and the resettlement of rural America all stand out as prominent themes in this ambitious vision for recovering a livable, humane economy that values persons over work. Cobb has argued for self-sufficiency in many writings,[30] arguing that self-sufficient economies are less dependent on foreign oil, the glut of consumer goods that saturate international markets, and the machinations of global finance that increase the wealth of the privileged at the expense of the poorest inhabitants of the planet. He has invoked a tentative comparison between his own vision and that of feudalism, acknowledging the problematic implications of that term. The stress here is consistently local: keeping the faces of workers in mind, valuing persons over labor, and the well-being of concrete communities rather than an amorphous global economy. His work as a visionary is hard to underestimate, and much within it directly echoes my own insistence on valuing workers over work. But at the same time, there are tendencies within this vision that seem to run counter to the boundary-breaking impetus of the Christian gospel. One question to ask Cobb, then, is whether his vision of local economic life serves to break down the barriers that separate human persons by nation, race, religion, and ethnicity. Is the neo-feudal vision of the local economy consistent with a reign in which there is no Jew or Greek, slave or free, male and female (Gal. 3:28), a reign that beckons the possibility of transnational community? Or does it simply keep each self-sufficient community in its own backyard?

Cobb has compared his vision with the Roman Catholic principle of subsidiarity.[31] But there are some subtle differences between a strong stress on local economies with this core principle of Catholic social teaching, a principle that the working world needs to hear afresh. Though it has roots in earlier papal documents and theological traditions, the classic statement of subsidiarity is found in Pius XI's *Quadragesimo Anno* (1931):

> It is indeed true, as history clearly shows, that owing to the change in social conditions, much that was formerly done by small bodies can nowadays be accomplished only by large organizations. Nevertheless, it is a fundamental principle of social philosophy, fixed and unchangeable, that one should not withdraw from individuals and commit to the community what they can accomplish by their own enterprise and industry. So, too, it is an injustice and at the same time a grave evil and a disturbance of right order to transfer to the larger and higher collectivity functions which can be performed and provided for by lesser and subordinate bodies. Inasmuch as every social activity should, by its very nature, prove a help to members of the body social, it should never destroy or absorb them.[32]

The history of this principle has experienced vagaries of interpretation: conservatives have invoked it as a defense of laissez-faire governance. Clearly, the principle does suggest that larger collectives such as the State should not arrogate the responsibilities and roles of local communities. Yet stressing the neofederalist themes of the document amounts to selective attention, for the encyclical also claims that every social activity should serve as a help to the common good that transcends local and national boundaries. In this regard, subsidiarity neither endorses the principle that the local alone is sufficient, nor abrogates the local in favor of larger, faceless collectives.

John Paul Szura claims that the principle simply speaks to the "profound drive in human beings to seek from others the help needed to become or do something."[33] To be a human person is to seek out others: we grow into fuller personhood as we are supported by others in communities such as the family, friendships, churches, communities, and governments. The principle of subsidiarity, then, does not endorse the concept of "less government is better," but acknowledges that those organizations closest to the faces of others are generally in the best position to assess the help necessary for communal flourishing. The function of local communities and institutions, then, is not to bolster the voice of the largest institutions, as if one's allegiance to the national government trumped all local interests. Rather, the drive is the reverse: larger, national institutions exist so that local communities may more fully flourish. The accountability structures, in other words, always flow back to the local faces and relationships that enable life in community.

The main difference between subsidiarity and the proposals of Cobb and Daly is that the former does not see globalization as an inherently problematic development. Whereas Cobb and Daly long for a return to local economies, there are some strands of globalization that might be welcomed, such as the growing capacity for workers' solidarity across national lines; the flow of goods, immunizations, and low-interest loans to regions heretofore outside marketplace loops; and the proliferation of communication across cultural divides made possible by accessible communication technologies. Invoking subsidiarity, in other words, does not result in an explicitly antiglobal vision of work; indeed, some aspects of the global economy might be seen as dim echoes of Christian hopes for the reign of God, such as when barriers between nations crumble as borders open up and persons from nations at war with one another build a friendship via e-mail.

What would an implementation of subsidiarity mean for the economic life of nations? Pius XI suggests that it would involve a Christianization of the social order: moral renovation, the reinstitution of guilds, and a recovery of dogma at the heart of economic life. Looking back at his constructive proposals, they sound naïve and enormously problematic in religiously plural societies such as the Unitd States. Despite the weaknesses of his constructive proposals (which represent more a return to an older economic order than an outline of a new one), the main theme of subsidiarity still might be employed as an economic principle. The point is this: economic policies and movements must always be measured in terms of their impact on concrete, local communities and the dignity of workers as persons within those communities. Economic growth, in other words, cannot be justified if it has catastrophic implications on the workers who fuel the factories that produce growth. These are the very measures, however, that current arrangements of global economic policy seem to lack. Loan terms from the World Bank, for example, assign the highest interest rates to the poorest nations because they are higher-risk lenders. Such interest rates, we are told, make for sound economic policy. The results, however, have been devastating for citizens of those poor nations, who have seen debts skyrocket, government services plummet, and life expectancy and health care decline. While global prosperity rises with the acceleration of global capital flow, the poorest of the poor, who experience most directly the impact of transnational financial institutions such as the World Bank, suffer inordinately because of "prosperity" elsewhere. The principle of subsidiarity, by contrast, would acknowledge the need for transnational financial institutions, but measure their impact in terms of the local faces who are the indirect recipients of these loans. Two alternatives using this principle are possible: forgiveness of the loans themselves, or the lowering of interest rates in ways that fly in the face of market logic, so that higher-risk poorer nations pay less interest than their wealthier counterparts who can more easily afford it.[34]

Subsidiarity does not offer a blueprint for global economic life. It does not represent a constructive alternative to global capitalism or attempts at socialism; rather, it serves as a measurement of the human impact of economic systems that current global systems lack. It is quite possible that the principle itself could be compatible—given enough systemic readjustment—with some visions of global capitalism or more socialist renderings of economic life.[35] The principle reminds us that the chief measure of economic growth is the lives of the human persons that make growth possible. The health of a society, in other words, is most appropriately measured not by abstract statistics on growth, job creation, and income levels, but on the quality of life of human persons, created in God's image.

This recognition is echoed in the U.S. bishop's letter on economic life: "*The dignity of the human person, realized in community with others, is the criterion against which all aspects of economic life must be measured.*"[36] Work has meaning not because it stokes the engines of consumer society, not because work is the labor by which we create ourselves, but because human persons do work.[37] Work has value in the global economy because persons in God's image respond to the work God has already accomplished. The measure of good work and economic systems, therefore, must always be measured in terms of their impact on the worker: Does the system enable the network of relationships that are essential for human flourishing to grow, including our relationship with the earth? Does the growth of the economy include increased networks of help and mutual accountability that promote human flourishing? Does the work that is needed in the global economy serve to dignify or disparage the worker? Do workers experience their work as owned by others or as outlets for their own expression and creativity? Do the engines of economic growth seek the gifts of all persons as workers or only those fortunate enough to benefit from the New World Order? Do our labors foster a connection to the land and a sense of private property that accentuates rather than neglects the common good? Our answers to these questions reveal much about the ordering of economic life, our attitude toward work, and whether we value workers as persons or as pawns to economic growth.

The Reformed tradition has its own understanding of ordering the household: the covenant. God establishes covenant with particular people not to the exclusion of others in the household, but so that God's promise of life takes flesh in particular faces in history. As the Presbyterian Brief Statement of Faith puts it, "In everlasting love, the God of Abraham and Sarah chose a covenant people to bless all families of the earth." These promises to Israel are extended to the world in Jesus Christ, who makes us heirs to the covenant. Though the initiator of this covenant is always God, Reformed Christianity has also stressed the response of God's people. Though God claims us despite our unworthiness, God also calls us to live into covenantal promises, in life and in work as we regard *all others* as covenant people: "In sovereign love, God created the world good and makes everyone equally in God's image, male and female, of every race and people, to live as one community."[38] Like the principle of subsidiarity, covenant stresses mutual accountability. We live out of God's promises and respond to them, in no small part, in our relationships with other people. Love of God is a mere platitude until it is put into action in human community. Hearkening Catholic themes of subsidiarity only amplifies strands within Reformed Christianity that already stress covenantal promises of life as one community, dismantling walls of prejudice and self-interest. We work in economic systems not for our own gain, but for a reign that comes through God's work. Our efforts will not bring about the reign, but they do offer one form of response, one eruption of thanks and praise to the One whose work only ceases when God will be all in all. Human labor, too, can be one expression of praise, but for that praise to be heard, the household must also be attentive to the working gifts of all God's creatures. Surely, that is work worth pursuing, even unto the ends of the earth.

Notes

Preface

1. Thankfully, some exceptions to this absence of reflection on work in doctrinal theology have emerged in recent decades. Some of the more significant are Dorothee Soelle with Shirley A. Cloyes, *To Work and to Love: A Theology of Creation* (Philadelphia: Fortress Press, 1984); Miroslav Volf, *Work in the Spirit: Toward a Theology of Work* (New York: Oxford University Press, 1991); M. Douglas Meeks, *God the Economist: The Doctrine of God and Political Economy* (Minneapolis: Fortress Press, 1989); R. Paul Stevens, *The Other Six Days: Vocation, Work, and Ministry in Biblical Perspective* (Grand Rapids and Vancouver: Eerdmans and Regent, 2000), Douglas J. Schuurman, *Vocation: Discerning Our Callings in Life* (Grand Rapids: Eerdmans, 2004), Lee Hardy, *The Fabric of This World: Inquiries into Calling, Career Choice, and the Design of Human Work* (Grand Rapids: Eerdmans, 1990), and Armand Larive, *After Sunday: A Theology of Work* (New York: Continuum, 2004).

Chapter 1: Life's Labors

1. The phrases "work to live" and "live to work" are inspired by an essay by Dorothy Sayers, "Why Work?" in *Creed or Chaos?* (New York: Harcourt, Brace, and Company, 1949), 53: "Work is not, primarily, a thing one does to live, but the thing one lives to do."
2. Soelle, *To Work and to Love*, 60.
3. Horace Bushnell, "Work and Play," *Horace Bushnell: Sermons*, ed. Conrad Cherry (New York: Paulist Press, 1985), 74.
4. Al Gini, *My Job My Self: Work and the Creation of the Modern Individual* (New York: Routledge, 2000), 15–16.
5. Richard Higginson, *Mind the Gap: Connecting Faith with Work* (Warwick, England: CPAS, 1997), 7.
6. Miroslav Volf offers an even more specific understanding of work: "Work is honest, purposeful, and methodologically specified social activity whose primary goal is the creation of products or states of affairs that can satisfy the

123

needs of working individuals or their co-creatures, or (if primarily an end in itself) activity that is necessary for acting individuals to satisfy their needs apart from the need for the activity itself." *Work in the Spirit: Toward a Theology of Work* (New York: Oxford, 1991), 10–11. As valuable as Volf's definition is, it lacks the rather concise nature of work as "activity undertaken with a sense of obligation."

7. This sense of obligation is critical for understanding an activity as work, and helps us distinguish between work and play. Not all activities that build and maintain relationships qualify as work. Lovemaking, for example, is an activity for the sake of another and oneself that sustains and nourishes an intimate relationship, but hardly qualifies as work. The absence of obligation, in this case, seems to be key: when one makes love out of a sense of obligation, the activity ceases to be lovemaking and becomes a mechanical act devoid of happiness and intimacy. Lovemaking is spontaneous and has no goal other than the sharing of pleasure, happiness, play, and connection with the beloved. As play, its significance is found in the activity itself, not in an end. By contrast, there are other activities, undertaken for the sake of building and maintaining relationships in the family, that surely qualify as work: when I volunteer for the PTA at my daughter's school, for example, I undertake this activity, at least in part, out of a sense of obligation to my daughter, her fellow students, and the teachers at the neighborhood school. The presence or absence of obligation helps us determine whether a specific human activity is more adequately described as work or play.

8. Frederick Buechner defines vocation as "the place where your deep gladness meets the world's deep need." *Wishful Thinking: A Seeker's ABC* (San Francisco: HarperSanFrancisco, 1993), 119.

9. Meeks, *God the Economist*, 171.

10. Bureau of Labor Statistics, United States Department of Labor, "The Unemployment Situation: April 2005" (Washington: U.S. Department of Labor, 2005), 1. Just prior to Hurricane Katrina in August 2005, the jobless rate dipped below 5 percent, though the aftereffects of that cataclysm caused a significant upsurge in the ranks of the unemployed.

11. The term "natural rate" is often attributed to the work of Milton Friedman. For analysis of the natural rate, see Joseph Stiglitz, "Reflections on the Natural Rate Hypothesis," *The Journal of Economic Perspectives* 11, no. 1 (Winter 1997): 3–10. Yet the natural rate is hardly an unquestioned datum of modern economic thought. For alternative perspectives see Richard S. Krashevski, "What Is So Natural about High Unemployment?" *The American Economic Review* 78, no. 2 (May 1988): 289–93, and Richard Rogerson, "Theory Ahead of Language in the Economics of Unemployment," *The Journal of Economic Perspectives* 11, no. 1 (Winter 1997): 73–92. Brian Peterson helped me understand the concept of "natural rate," and noted its contestability in current discussions of unemployment.

12. Bureau of Labor Statistics, "The Unemployment Situation: April 2005," 8.

13. Wilson, cited in Gini, *My Job*, 188.

14. Soelle, *To Work and to Love*, 69.

15. Bureau of Labor Statistics, "The Unemployment Situation: April 2005," 3.

16. Lawrence Mishel, Jared Bernstein, and Sylvia Allegretto, *The State of Working America 2004/2005* (Ithaca, NY: Cornell University Press, 2005), 246–48. If these 2.5 million "missing workers" were included in current statistics, the unemployment rate would be more than 7 percent. Ibid., 8.

17. Bureau of Labor Statistics, United States Department of Labor, "Employment Characteristics of Families in 2003" (Washington, DC: U.S. Department of Labor, 2004), 1.
18. Ibid., 2.
19. Meeks, *God the Economist*, 174.
20. I explore this theme of God's superfluous self-giving and its relation to human work in chapter 3.
21. Bureau of Labor Statistics, U.S. Department of Labor, *A Profile of the Working Poor, 2003*, Report 983 (Washington, DC: U.S. Department of Labor, 2005), 1.
22. Mishel et al., *State of Working America*, 313.
23. Ibid. Barbara Ehrenreich's groundbreaking study *Nickel and Dimed: On (Not) Getting By in America* (New York: Henry Holt and Company, 2001), documents the physical and mental exhaustion of the lowest-wage occupations of our consumer-driven economy.
24. Bureau of Labor Statistics, *Profile of the Working Poor*, 1–3.
25. The phrase "second shift" is from Arlie Russel Hochschild's *The Second Shift* (New York: Penguin Books, 1989).
26. Mishel, Bernstein, and Allegretto note that "the industries that are expanding [in the United States] . . . pay far less in wages, benefits, and total compensation than industries that are contracting" (*State of Working America*, 28.)
27. Bureau of Labor Statistics, U.S. Department of Labor. http://stats.bls.gov/cps/minwage2004.htm.
28. Bureau of Labor Statistics, U.S. Department of Labor, http://stats.bls.gov/cps/minwage2004tbls.htm.
29. Mishel et al., *State of Working America*, 32. "The U.S. economy has been consistently expanding for years, yet real wages of the middle-class working Americans have been falling, and virtually all of the growth that has occurred has flowed to profits, not labor" (17).
30. Ibid., 214.
31. I explore these eucharistic themes of work in chapter 4.
32. I explore Marx in more detail in chapter 2.
33. www.conferenceboard.org/utilities/pressDetail.cfm?press_ID=2582.
34. Lee Hardy warns against making job satisfaction the primary criterion for meaningful work, in part, because it places the self at the center of the understanding of vocation. Satisfaction, he claims, "cannot, for the Christian, serve as the sole or even primary criterion by which a job is evaluated. For an occupation must be first considered in terms of how it provides a fitting place for the exercise of one's gift in the service of others" (*The Fabric of This World: Inquiries into Calling, Career Choice, and the Design of Human Work* [Grand Rapids: Eerdmans, 1990], 98). Though I, too, would be wary of making satisfaction the sole determinant of fulfilling work (no doubt many have found satisfaction in destructive, and even criminal, forms of human labor), personal satisfaction is not irrelevant to vocation and meaningful work. One obviously can perform socially useful and Christian-like service wholly begrudgingly. If one with an attitude of drudgery performs work that serves others, is good work really being done? A larger sense of meaningful work hearkens Frederick Buechner's dictum that vocation is where the heart's deep gladness meets the world's deep need. Surely gladness is a result of some degree of satisfaction in work.

35. Colin Allen, "Rank Determines Job Satisfaction," *Psychology Today* (October 6, 2003), http://cms.psychologytoday.com/articles/index.php. See also Gordon D. A. Brown, Jonathan Gardner, Andrew Oswald, and Jing Qian, "Rank Dependence in Pay Satisfaction," unpublished paper presented at the Warwick-Brookings conference, Washington, DC, June 5–6, 2003.

36. Bureau of Labor Statistics, U.S. Department of Labor, "Issues in Labor Statistics," Summary 99–10, September 1999, 1.

37. Al Gini, *The Importance of Being Lazy: In Praise of Play, Leisure, and Vacations* (New York: Routledge, 2003), 16.

38. Karl Marx, "Estranged Labor," in Dirk J. Struik, ed., *The Economic and Philosophic Manuscripts of 1844* (New York: International Publishers, 1964), 110.

39. Hauntingly, the slogan emblazoned on the iron gates of the Dachau concentration camp is *"Arbeit macht frei"* (work makes one free).

40. http://archives.cnn.com/2001/CAREER/trends/08/30/ilo.study.

41. Gini, *My Job My Self*, 86.

42. Marilyn Gardner, "More Working Parents Play 'Beat the Clock,'" *The Christian Science Monitor,* June 2, 2004, www.csmonitor.com/2004/0602/p11s02-lifp.htm.

43. Mishel et al., *State of Working America*, 100–101.

44. Cindy Krischer Goodman, "Overwhelmed Employees Suffer More Than Mere Exhaustion," *The Houston Chronicle*, April 16, 2005, www.chron.com/cs/CDA/printstory.mpl/business/3137829.

45. Witold Rybczynski, *Waiting for the Weekend* (New York: Viking, 1991), 215.

46. Juliet B. Schor, *The Overworked American: The Unexpected Decline of Leisure* (New York: Basic Books, 1992), 47.

47. Ibid., 43–48.

48. Ibid., 2.

49. Mishel et al., *State of Working America*, 388. Worker productivity in the United States grew 72 percent from 1973 to 2003 (p. 149).

50. Sayers, *Creed or Chaos?* 46.

51. Rosalind Chait Barnett, "Reduced Hours Work/Part-time Work," in ed., Marcie Pitt-Catsouphes and Ellen Kossek, *Sloan Work and Family Encyclopedia*, http://.wfnetwork.bc.edu/encyclopedia.php?mode=nau&area=academics.

52. For an exposé on the male phenomenon of workaholism and dependence on work, as well as pastoral reflections on recovering more spiritually grounded practices of work, see James E. Dittes, *Men at Work: Life beyond the Office* (Louisville, KY: Westminster John Knox Press, 1996).

53. I explore these themes more fully in chapter 4, where I consider worship as "work of the people" and as rest from our labors.

54. Arlie Russell Hochschild, *The Time Bind: When Work Becomes Home and Home Becomes Work* (New York: Owl Books, 1997).

55. Bureau of Labor Statistics, U.S. Department of Labor, "Women in the Labor Force: A Databook" (Washington, DC: U.S. Department of Labor, 2005), 1.

56. Bureau of Labor Statistics, U.S. Department of Labor, "Time-Use Survey—First Results Announced by BLS" (Washington, DC: U.S. Department of Labor, 2004), 1–3.

57. Hochschild, *Second Shift*, 285–92.

58. David Lyman, "Vacation? No Thanks, Boss," *Austin American-Statesman*, July 12, 2004, E1. In the same article one municipal worker talks about being "married" to the City of Austin; here, the workplace becomes a kind of intimate partner, a substitute for a human partnership.

59. Gini, *Importance of Being Lazy*, 25.
60. Bureau of Labor Statistics, "Time-Use Survey," 3.
61. For further reflections on the theological significance of play, see David H. Jensen, *Graced Vulnerability: A Theology of Childhood* (Cleveland: Pilgrim Press, 2005), 54–58.
62. Gini, *Importance of Being Lazy*, 92.
63. Gini offers a striking exposé of our shopping culture and the disease of "affluenza," or the insatiable desire to have more, in ibid., 81–100.
64. John Calvin, *Institutes of the Christian Religion* 3.7.1; ed. John T. McNeill, trans. Ford Lewis Battles, LCC (Philadelphia: Westminster Press, 1960).

Chapter 2: Redeemed and Unredeemed Work

1. Here I differ from the recent work of Kathryn Tanner, who writes: "God after all is very rarely thought by Christian theologians to make the world through labor: God speaks, and the world immediately comes to be, without any effort, without materials or tools. God, in short, just does not work, and therefore the effort God expends, the work that God puts into it, cannot be the justification for God's ownership of the world" (*Economy of Grace* [Minneapolis: Fortress, 2005], 47). Critical as Tanner's points are for a reinterpretation of work—"hard work" does not justify ownership—they seem to remove God from work unnecessarily. The two creation narratives, upon close reading, depict God creating through speech *and* through work. In the first, God creates by divine word, without work (Gen. 1); in the second, God creates by forming Adam from the dust of the ground and planting a garden (Gen. 2:7–8). The rhythms of work and rest, it seems, are bound up with divine creativity.
2. Meeks, *God the Economist*, 146. Meeks also offers a pointed analysis of how monarchial images of God contribute to the denigration of human work (135).
3. Mark and Matthew underscore the abrupt nature of this change by noting that the disciples "immediately" leave their nets and follow Jesus (Matt. 4:22; Mark 1:18).
4. In a similar vein, Genesis portrays humanity as eating meat subsequent to expulsion. Prior to that God gives humanity every "green plant" for food (1:30b). Might the omnivorous diet, which entails significantly more labor than vegetable diets, express some of the alienation of humanity from other species as well as its experience of alienation in work?
5. Karl Marx, "Das Kapital," in *Karl Marx Friedrich Engels Werke*, vol. 23 (Berlin: Dietz Verlag, 1962), 57, translation mine.
6. Miroslav Volf, *Work in the Spirit: Toward a Theology of Work* (London: Oxford University Press, 1991), 58.
7. For Marx, the only liberation from alienated work is rightly oriented work, a "kingdom of freedom" where work is the full expression of human personhood. Human work, when rightly oriented, and not owned by others, can provide the seeds of liberation. Where alienating work enslaves, humane work saves. We will explore this glorified view of work shortly.
8. Etienne Gilson, ed., *The Church Speaks to the Modern World: The Social Teachings of Leo XIII* (Garden City, NY: Doubleday & Company, 1954), 206–7.
9. *Rerum Novarum* issues an early call for a "living wage." "Wages ought not to be insufficient to support a frugal and well-behaved wage-earner" (ibid., 230).
10. Ibid., 227–28.

11. "Too early an experience of life's hard toil blight[s] the young promise of a child's faculties, and render[s] any true education impossible" (ibid., 228).
12. *The Rule of St. Benedict*, trans. Anthony C. Meisel and M. L. del Mastro (Garden City, NY: Image Books, 1975), 86.
13. Ibid., 87.
14. Ibid., 77.
15. William of St. Thierry, *The Golden Epistle*, trans. Theodore Berkeley (Kalamazoo, MI: Cistercian Publications, 1971), 39.
16. Ibid.
17. Ibid., 40.
18. Ibid.
19. James Walsh, S.J., *The Cloud of Unknowing* (Mahwah, NJ: Paulist Press, 1981), 156–58.
20. Max Weber, *The Protestant Ethic and the "Spirit" of Capitalism and Other Writings*, ed. Peter Baehr and Gordon C. Wells (New York: Penguin, 2002), 115.
21. Ibid., 116.
22. Martin Luther, "The Judgment of Martin Luther on Monastic Vows," in *Luther's Works*, vol. 44, ed. James Atkinson (Philadelphia: Fortress Press, 1966), 334.
23. Luther, "Commentary on 1 Corinthians 7," in *Works*, vol. 28, ed. Hilton C. Oswald (St. Louis: Concordia Publishing House, 1973), 20.
24. Luther's extensive writings on justification, for example, cannot be read apart from his intense concern with the practical implications of this doctrine: how one lives out Christian faith and the security of Christian life in a broken world. Justification meant that one could entrust one's life to God and not to oneself. Trusting in God, one is free to do good work without attaching oneself to that work.
25. Luther, "The Estate of Marriage," in *Works*, vol. 45, ed. Walther I. Brandt (Philadelphia: Fortress Press, 1962), 40.
26. Luther, "Notes on Ecclesiastes," in *Works*, vol. 15, ed. Jaroslav Pelikan (St. Louis: Concordia, 1972), 98, emphasis mine.
27. This conviction helps explain Luther's notorious polemics against the Peasants' Rebellion. Their struggle, Luther claimed, represented a defiance of the orders of creation and God's call on the unique stations of peasants' lives. See Luther, "An Open Letter on the Harsh Book Against the Peasants," in *Works*, vol. 46, ed. Robert C. Schultz (Philadelphia: Fortress Press, 1967), 63–85.
28. Calvin, *Institutes* 3.10.6.
29. Ibid.
30. Ibid., 3.14.9.
31. Ibid., 3.11.13.
32. Parker J. Palmer, *Let Your Life Speak: Listening for the Voice of Vocation* (San Francisco: Jossey-Bass, 2000), 10.
33. Douglas J. Schuurman, *Vocation: Discerning Our Callings in Life* (Grand Rapids: Eerdmans, 2004), xiii.
34. Ibid., 79.
35. Since 1999, the Eli Lilly Endowment, for example, has granted eighty-eight U.S. colleges and universities "Theological Exploration of Vocation" grants that total $171.3 million. These grants are designed to nurture students' theological reflection on faith and vocational choices. See www.lillyendowment.org/religion_ptev.html.

36. Volf claims as much in *Work in the Spirit*, opting for an understanding of work as charisma rather than vocation. See pp. 102–19.
37. "Slavery contradicts Christianity because it is contrary to reason." Peter C. Hodgson, ed., *Hegel Lectures on the Philosophy of Religion: One-Volume Edition, The Lectures of 1827* (Berkeley: University of California Press, 1988), 482.
38. G. W. F. Hegel, *Phenomenology of Spirit*, trans. A. V. Miller (Oxford: Oxford University Press, 1977), 213.
39. Karl Marx, *The Grundrisse*, ed. David McLellan (New York: Harper & Row, 1971), 124.
40. The closest recent theological analogue to these voices is Matthew Fox's *The Reinvention of Work: A New Vision of Livelihood for Our Time* (San Francisco: HarperCollins, 1994), which invokes strains of liberation along the lines of revisionist sacramentology. "We are graced by the universe. Its work is sacramental, a revelation of divine grace. Therefore, our work—to the extent that it joins the Great Work of the universe—is also a sacrament" (17). "The most important work of our time is *work on the human species itself.* This is how we will both reinvent work and redeem the work worlds in which we operate" (297).
41. John Paul II, "Laborem Exercens," in *The Encyclicals of John Paul II*, ed. J. Michael Miller (Huntington, IN: Our Sunday Visitor, 1996), 180–81.
42. Ibid., 171.
43. Ibid., 212.
44. Armand Larive, *After Sunday: A Theology of Work* (New York: Continuum, 2004), 155.
45. Ibid., 88.
46. Volf, *Work in the Spirit*, 98.
47. Ibid., 114.

Chapter 3: God's Work for Us

1. Gregory of Nyssa, "An Answer to Ablabius," in *Christology of the Later Fathers*, ed. Edward R. Hardy (Philadelphia: Westminster, 1954), 259.
2. For this expression I am indebted to Edward Farley, who argues for an approach to the question of God that privileges "the faith and experience of a specific and actual people." God comes forth as God as the redeemer of the human condition in ecclesial communities. Farley, *Divine Empathy: A Theology of God* (Minneapolis: Fortress Press, 1996), 20.
3. Thomas Aquinas, *Summa Theologiae* (New York and London: McGraw-Hill and Eyre & Spottiswoode, 1964), 1, q.13, a.5.
4. Sallie McFague, *Life Abundant: Rethinking Theology and Economy for a Planet in Peril* (Minneapolis: Fortress Press, 2001), 183.
5. James Francis, "God as Worker: A Metaphor from Daily Life in Biblical Perspective," in *Metaphor, Canon and Community: Jewish, Christian and Islamic Approaches*, ed. Ralph Bisschops and James Francis (New York: Peter Lang, 1999), 16.
6. See also Jer. 9:7: "Therefore thus says the LORD of hosts: I will now refine and test them, for what else can I do with my sinful people?"
7. Marc Kolden, "Work and Meaning: Some Theological Reflections," *Interpretation* 48 (July 1994): 263.
8. The neologism "gifting" comes from Stephen H. Webb, *The Gifting God: A Trinitarian Ethics of Excess* (New York: Oxford University Press, 1996).

9. Karl Rahner, *The Trinity*, trans. Joseph Donceel (New York: Crossroad, 1999), 10–11.

10. Catherine LaCugna, `God for Us: The Trinity and Christian Life` (San Francisco: HarperCollins, 1991), ix.

11. Here I am confronted by the challenge of what language to use in expressing God's self-communicating goodness and love. Multiple strands of Christian tradition have bequeathed us the language of Father, Son, and Holy Spirit, words as evocative as they are alienating. Recognizing that no name for God can ever fully express the fullness of God's gift and self-communicating love, and affirming with feminist theologians that traditional Trinitarian language for God may fail to express the communion that lies behind patriarchal language, I use here the classical Father-Son-Holy Spirit imagery as well as alternative formulations, such as Creator-Redeemer-Sustainer, and God-Word-Spirit. Each formulation has its shortcomings, whether patriarchal or modalist.

12. Meeks, *God the Economist*, 132–33.

13. By invoking these biblical texts, I am not attempting to force them into a Trinitarian mold. Rather, I am showing how the varied biblical images for God's work point not to a parceling out of divine tasks, but the sharing of distinct and abundant work.

14. Calvin, *Institutes* 1.13.17.

15. Ibid., 1.13.18.

16. Full employment, sometimes referred to as the "natural rate," is highly contested in economic theory (see chapter 1, note 11). For some economists, full employment means an unemployment rate as low as 2.5%, while for others that number may reach as high as 7%. The usage of the term "full employment" in this study, however, runs against most hypotheses of the natural rate. Full employment, as I employ the term, means nothing less than paid work for all persons who seek it.

17. If economic productivity is the chief marker of personhood, then not only are the unemployed considered less than full persons, but so too are the elderly and children. For a view of children as gift, see David H. Jensen, *Graced Vulnerability: A Theology of Childhood* (Cleveland: Pilgrim Press, 2005), 35–63, and Bonnie J. Miller-McLemore, *Let the Children Come: Reimagining Childhood from a Christian Perspective* (San Francisco: Jossey-Bass, 2003), 83–104.

18. I explore some of the systemic economic implications of this theological view of work in chapter 5.

19. Gregory of Nazianzus, "The Theological Orations," in Hardy, ed., *Christology of the Later Fathers*, 171.

20. Gregory of Nyssa, "An Answer to Alabius," in ibid., 261–62.

21. The Second Helvetic Confession echoed these patristic themes in the Reformation period: "Thus there are not three gods, but three persons, consubstantial, coeternal, and coequal; distinct with respect to hypostases, and with respect to order, the one preceding the other yet without any inequality. For according to the nature or essence they are so joined together that they are one God, and the divine nature is common to the Father, Son and Holy Spirit." *The Constitution of the Presbyterian Church (U.S.A.)*, part 1, *The Book of Confessions* (Louisville, KY: Presbyterian Church (U.S.A.), 1996), 5.017.

22. Meeks, *God the Economist*, 133.

23. Gregory of Nazianzus, "Theological Orations," in Hardy, ed., *Christology of the Later Fathers*, 172.

24. LaCugna, *God for Us*, 69.
25. Gregory of Nyssa, "Answer to Alabius," in Hardy, ed., *Christology of the Later Fathers*, 262.
26. Ibid., 263.
27. Kathryn Tanner, *Jesus, Humanity, and the Trinity: A Brief Systematic Theology* (Minneapolis: Fortress Press, 2001), 39.
28. Athanasius, "Orations against the Arians, Book I," in *The Trinitarian Controversy*, ed. William G. Rusch (Philadelphia: Fortress Press, 1980), 109. J. N. D. Kelly interprets Gregory of Nyssa along similar lines: "The divine action begins from the Father, proceeds through the Son, and is completed in the Holy Spirit; none of the Persons possesses a separate operation of His own, but one identical energy passes through all Three" (*Early Christian Doctrines*, rev. ed. [San Francisco: HarperSanFrancisco, 1978], 267).
29. Speaking of U.S. economic recovery since 2001, the writers of *The State of Working America* note: "The lack of job creation in this latest recovery has been unprecedented, which is why the recovery was deemed a 'jobless' one. A jobless recovery occurs when an economy begins to expand (as defined by the National Bureau of Economic Research) but businesses continue to shed jobs," 219.
30. For a similar analysis of workfare and its divergence from the divine economy, see Tanner, *Economy of Grace*, 99–105.
31. I explore the theme of full employment in more detail in chapter 5.
32. Peter C. Hodgson, ed., *Hegel Lectures on the Philosophy of Religion*, 434.
33. "This other, released as something free and independent, is *the world* as such," ibid.
34. G. W. F. Hegel, "Phenomenology of Spirit," in *G. W. F. Hegel: Theologian of the Spirit*, ed. Peter C. Hodgson (Minneapolis: Fortress Press, 1997), 94.
35. *Book of Confessions*, 7.001.
36. Rahner, *The Trinity*, 21.
37. Athanasius, "Orations against the Arians," 110.
38. LaCugna, *God for Us*, 228.
39. Tanner, *Jesus, Humanity, and the Trinity*, 41. "God from the start is giving all God can but the creature from the start cannot receive it" (42.)
40. See also Volf, *Work in the Spirit*, 89–102.
41. Meeks, *God the Economist*, 149.
42. Catherine LaCugna offers a vision of the end of human being, along the lines cited in this chapter: "*The freedom of the deified human being consists in being free-for, free-toward others, poised in the balance between self-possession and other-orientation*" (*God for Us*, 290). The freedom of the human person is not expressed in autonomy or heteronomy, but in being freed for relation with God, oneself, others, and the earth itself. Freedom in work occurs when work is an expression of these relationships given us by God.

Chapter 4: Work of the People

1. *The Constitution of the Presbyterian Church (U.S.A.), part 2: Book of Order* (Louisville, KY: Presbyterian Church (U.S.A.), 1997), W-6.003.
2. See Justin Martyr, "The First Apology of Justin," in *The Ante-Nicene Fathers*, vol. 1, ed. Alexander Roberts and James Donaldson (Grand Rapids: Eerdmans, 1950), 185–86, and Gordon Lathrop's commentary in *Holy Things: A Liturgical Theology* (Minneapolis: Fortress Press, 1993), 45–46.

3. Alexander Schmemann, *For the Life of the World* (Crestwood, NY: St. Vladimir's Seminary Press, 1988), 25.

4. David Buttrick, "Liturgy, Reformed," in *The Westminster Handbook to Reformed Theology*, ed. Donald K. McKim (Louisville, KY: Westminster John Knox Press, 2001), 139.

5. Calvin, *Institutes* 4.17.44.

6. Ibid., 4.14.1. The Second Helvetic Confession offers an analogous definition: "Sacraments are mystical symbols, or holy rites, or sacred actions, instituted by God himself, consisting of his Word, of signs and of things signified, whereby in the Church he keeps in mind and from time to time recalls the great benefits he has shown to men; whereby also he seals his promises, and outwardly represents, and, as it were, offers unto our sight those things which inwardly he performs for us, and so strengthens and increases our faith through the working of God's Spirit in our hearts" (*Book of Confessions*, 5.169).

7. Calvin, *Institutes* 4.17.1.

8. "There is in every sacrament a spiritual relation, or sacramental union, between the sign and the thing signified." Westminster Confession, *Book of Confessions*, 6.150. The bread of Holy Communion, in Reformed thinking, represents food for a world that is physically and spiritually starving. Indeed, there is no strict separation between "spiritual" and "physical" needs in this understanding, because a union exists between the sign and the thing signified. Christ gives us his body and blood so that we may no longer hunger and thirst.

9. Robert W. Jenson, "Sacraments of the Word," in *Christian Dogmatics*, vol. 2, ed. Carl E. Braaten and Robert W. Jenson (Philadelphia: Fortress Press, 1984), 310.

10. Volf, *Work in the Spirit*, 136–37.

11. "Protestant principle" is Paul Tillich's phrase. See Tillich, *Systematic Theology*, vol. 1 (Chicago: The University of Chicago Press, 1951), 37.

12. Schmemann, *The Eucharist: Sacrament of the Kingdom*, trans. Paul Kachur (Crestwood, NY: St. Vladimir's Seminary Press, 1987), 19.

13. Ibid., 61.

14. Joseph Cardinal Ratzinger (Benedict XVI), *God and the World: Believing and Living in Our Time*, trans. Henry Taylor (San Francisco: Ignatius Press, 2002), 412.

15. The Johannine text is suggestive here. In the first resurrection appearance, Jesus tells Mary, "Do not hold on to me, because I have not yet ascended to the Father" (John 20:17a). No longer bound by the flesh, the risen Christ cannot be grabbed as if he were for the disciples alone. Because he gives himself for the world, he cannot be contained. His body has transitioned from a local, physical presence to a spiritual body that infuses the world.

16. Pierre Teilhard de Chardin, *The Divine Milieu* (New York: Harper & Row, 1968), 64.

17. Ibid., 126.

18. Gordon W. Lathrop, *Holy Ground: A Liturgical Cosmology* (Minneapolis: Fortress Press, 2003), 125.

19. Hochschild, *Second Shift*, 10.

20. Many of us, however, experience church as yet another demand on one's time. Committee meetings, fellowship suppers, Sunday school teaching, and even church retreats—if they mimic the demands of workplace time—can be plugged into an overscheduled Palm Pilot just as easily as a business lunch. Meanwhile,

some manuals of church growth offer sound-bite wisdom attuned to corporate culture. See Lyle E. Schaller, *44 Ways to Increase Church Attendance* (Nashville: Abingdon Press, 1988). Corporate America, likewise, has become adept at co-opting Jesus as the model executive. See Laurie Beth Jones, *Jesus, CEO: Using Ancient Wisdom for Visionary Leadership* (New York: Hyperion, 1995).

21. Lathrop, *Holy Things: A Liturgical Theology* (Minneapolis: Fortress Press, 1993), 39.
22. *Book of Common Worship* (Louisville, KY: Westminster John Knox Press, 1993), 70–71.
23. See Schmemann, *Eucharist*, 163.
24. Nicholas K. Apostola, "Labor and Rest in the Context of a Christian Perspective on the Economy," *St. Vladimir's Theological Quarterly* 39, no. 2 (1995): 190.
25. Christian worship celebrates in the sacraments these basic things of life: bread broken for the world, wine poured for the forgiveness of sin, water splashed in a promise of rebirth, flesh bathed in baptismal water—all pointing to work of the people that becomes God's work.
26. Lathrop, *Holy Things*, 91.
27. See Apostola, "Labor and Rest," 194–95, for similar reflections on how the elements of the Eucharist stand as "symbols of the cooperation between us and God for our own sustenance and the transformation of the world."
28. Lathrop, *Holy Things*, 91.
29. Teilhard, *Divine Milieu*, 67.
30. Schmemann, *Eucharist*, 118. See also Lathrop, *Holy Things*, 93: "Before the liturgy even begins, as the food is brought and set out on an offertory table or credence or prothesis, a Christian may rightly behold the loaf and think, 'Here is all human life,' or see the wine, thinking, 'Here is the universe itself.'"
31. I explore these themes in greater detail in the next chapter.
32. Meister Eckhardt, quoted in Lathrop, *Holy Ground*, 150.
33. M. Shawn Copeland, "Body, Race, and Being," in *Constructive Theology: A Contemporary Approach to Classical Themes*, ed. Serene Jones and Paul Lakeland (Minneapolis: Fortress Press, 2005), 113.
34. Gustavo Gutiérrez has a similar view of the ordinary things at the Lord's Table: "The objects used in the Eucharist themselves recall that fellowship is rooted in God's will to give the goods of this earth to all persons so that they might build a more human world" (*A Theology of Liberation: History, Politics, and Salvation*, 15th anniversary ed., ed. Sister Caridad Inda and John Eagleson [Maryknoll, NY: Orbis Books, 1988], 149).
35. Richard R. Gaillardetz, *Transforming Our Days: Spirituality, Community, and Liturgy in a Technological Culture* (New York: Crossroad, 2000), 77.
36. Schmemann, *Eucharist*, 105.
37. Calvin, *Institutes* 4.17.3.
38. Schmemann, *Eucharist*, 90.
39. Schmemann, *Life of the World*, 45.
40. Stephen H. Webb, *The Gifting God: A Trinitarian Ethics of Excess* (New York: Oxford University Press, 1996), 93.
41. For a more thorough exploration of this kenotic theme as it relates to incarnation and the divine life, see David H. Jensen, *In the Company of Others: A Dialogical Christology* (Cleveland: Pilgrim Press, 2001), 74–89.
42. Gaillardetz, *Transforming Our Days*, 128–29.
43. Buttrick, *"Liturgy, Reformed,"* 139.

44. Augustine, *City of God*, trans. Henry Bettenson (New York: Penguin, 1972), 380.

45. The phrase "remember the future" is from Shirley Guthrie, *Christian Doctrine*, rev. ed. (Louisville, KY: Westminster John Knox Press, 1994), 385.

46. J. N. D. Kelly, *Early Christian Doctrines*, rev. ed. (San Francisco: HarperCollins, 1978), 450.

47. John Chrysostom, "Homily LXXXII," in *Nicene and Post-Nicene Fathers*, vol. 10, "Saint Chrysostom: Homilies on the Gospel of Saint Matthew" ed. Philip Schaff (Grand Rapids: Eerdmans, 1956), 495.

48. Victor Codina, "Sacraments," in *Mysterium Liberationis: Fundamental Concepts of Liberation Theology*, ed. Ignacio Ellacuría and Jon Sobrino (Maryknoll, NY: Orbis Books, 1993), 666–67.

49. Schmemann, *Eucharist*, 218–21.

50. Schmemann, *Life of the World*, 44.

51. See Calvin, *Institutes* 4.17.31. "They place Christ in the bread, while we do not think it lawful for us to drag him from heaven." Geoffrey W. Bromiley summarizes this pivotal Reformed doctrine rather well: "The Spirit unites things separated in space, raising us up to Christ, and making bread and wine our spiritual food and drink" ("Lord's Supper," in McKim, ed., *The Westminster Handbook to Reformed Theology*, 144).

52. Teilhard de Chardin, *Divine Milieu*, 72.

53. Ibid., 56.

54. Ibid., 61.

55. See Copeland, "Body, Race, and Being," in Jones and Lakeland, eds., *Constructive Theology*, 115.

56. The following exposition of Jesus' gestures of grace draw their initial impetus from "Four Gestures of Grace," a sermon preached by Rev. Stephen Hancock at Second Presbyterian Church, Nashville, Tennessee, on September 7, 1997. See also Nathan D. Mitchell, "Eucharist," in *New and Enlarged Handbook of Christian Theology*, ed. Donald W. Musser and Joseph L. Price (Nashville: Abingdon Press, 2003), 179.

57. Gaillardetz, *Transforming Our Days*, 112.

58. In this regard, the Saturn plant in Spring Hill, Tennessee, offers some hopeful signs of worker-management integration, though note the strong critique by Ken Estey in *A New Protestant Ethic at Work* (Cleveland: Pilgrim Press, 2002), 15–43.

Chapter 5: Working for a Living

1. The Bible, of course, is no stranger to this scenario; at the center of the Old Testament is the exodus of a displaced people out of slavery into freedom in a new land.

2. Cornel West, "Black Theology of Liberation as Critique of Capitalist Civilization," in James H. Cone & Gayraud S. Wilmore, *Black Theology: A Documentary History*, vol. 2: *1980–1992* (Maryknoll, NY: Orbis Books, 1993), 417.

3. West notes, "The first major industry to be revolutionized, the cotton industry, and hence to establish one of the early pillars of capitalist civilization, was built primarily upon the blood, sweat and tears of black people" (ibid., 423).

4. M. Douglas Meeks writes, "All democracies, in order to justify their existence, have interceded in the market with various measures to resist the rise of economic inequality. Despite the massive ideological thrust to the contrary, it was democratic government, not the market, that formed the middle-class and to

some extent gave access to it to the poor." From "Economy and the Future of Liberation Theology in North America," in *Liberating the Future: God, Mammon, and Theology*, ed. Joerg Rieger (Minneapolis: Fortress Press, 1998), 49.

5. See Estey, *A New Protestant Labor Ethic at Work*, 33–43.
6. See Volf, *Work in the Spirit*, 174–76.
7. Herman E. Daly & John B. Cobb Jr., *For the Common Good: Redirecting the Economy Toward Community, the Environment, and a Sustainable Future*, 2nd ed., (Boston: Beacon Press, 1994), 305.
8. Tanner, *Economy of Grace*, 25.
9. National Conference of Catholic Bishops, *Economic Justice for All: Pastoral Letter on Catholic Social Teaching and the U.S. Economy* (Washington, DC: United States Catholic Conference, 1986), 69.
10. Tanner, *Economy of Grace*, 75. "The theological principle of unconditional giving would intervene here to suggest welfare provision as a universal entitlement, sensitive only to need. Welfare provision should be considered a right of the needy, a matter of justice rather than a matter of voluntary largesse on the part of the privileged" (101).
11. For similar proposals, see ibid., 105.
12. See Michael Schut, ed., *Simpler Living, Compassionate Life: A Christian Perspective* (Denver: Living the Good News, 1999). At the same time that the movement to simplicity has gained wider attention, it has also become cleverly marketed. The underside of this hopeful movement is that it, too, can fall prey to voracious consumer appetites. Hence, we now can select from a dazzling array of slickly packaged simplicity magazines at the local mega-market, outfit our homes with high-priced "simple" furnishings, and use simplicity to feed our consumer cravings.
13. www.worktolive.info/poen_worl.cfm.
14. Mishel et al., *State of Working America*, 388.
15. One small-scale domestic example of incorporating Sabbath in corporate culture is the Chick-fil-A sandwich chain's practice of closing all restaurants on Sundays, in order that its employees might rest from the workweek, enjoy friends and family, or worship.
16. John B. Cobb Jr., *The Earthist Challenge to Economism: A Theological Critique of the World Bank* (New York: St. Martin's Press, 1999), 5.
17. Daly and Cobb, *For the Common Good*, 310. "During the past forty years, while the economy as measured by the GNP has more than doubled, the average rate of unemployment has risen sharply" (Cobb, *Sustainability: Economics, Ecology, and Justice* [Maryknoll, NY: Orbis Books, 1992], 61).
18. Mishel et al., *State of Working America*, 219–20.
19. Sallie McFague, *Life Abundant*, 80. "In calculating GDP, pollution is not only counted as a positive, but it may be done so three times: when an economic activity produces it, when it is cleaned up, and when associated health costs occur" (Barry Marquardson, "GDP Fails as a Measurement," *Globe and Mail*, July 16, 1998).
20. David Matzko McCarthy, *The Good Life: Genuine Christianity for the Middle Class* (Grand Rapids: Brazos Press, 2004), 121.
21. See McFague, *Life Abundant*, 113–14, for further discussion of the HDI and how it accounts for the relative health of societies.
22. Meeks, *God the Economist*, 57.
23. McCarthy, *Good Life*, 122.

24. *Rerum Novarum*, in Gilson, ed., *Church Speaks to the Modern World*, 209.
25. Ibid., 230.
26. "They learn to love the very soil that yields in response to the labor of their hands" (ibid., 231).
27. Theological indictments of global capitalism are legion. Examples of substantive critiques from a variety of perspectives include: West, "Black Theology of Liberation," in Cone and Wilmore, *Black Theology*; Riger, ed., *Liberating the Future*; Gutiérrez, *Theology of Liberation*; John Milbank, "The Body by Love Possessed: Christianity and Late Capitalism in Britain," *Modern Theology* 3, no. 1 (October 1986): 35–75; Ulrich Duchrow, "Private Property: A Growing Danger for Life (or: Neglected in the Globalization Debate)," *The Ecumenical Review* 54, no. 4 (October 2002): 472–82; D. Stephen Long, *Divine Economy: Theology and the Market* (New York: Routledge, 2000); Beverly Wildung Harrison, "The Role of Social Theory in Religious Social Ethics: Reconsidering the Case for Marxian Political Economy," in Harrison, *Making the Connections: Essays in Feminist Social Ethics*, ed. Carol S. Robb (Boston: Beacon Press, 1985), 54–80.
28. Daly and Cobb, *For the Common Good*, 6.
29. Mishel et al., *State of Working America*, 59.
30. Cobb, *Sustainability*, 70.
31. Daly and Cobb, *For the Common Good*, 16–17.
32. Pius XI, *Quadragesimo Anno*, in *Catholic Social Thought: The Documentary Heritage*, ed. David J. O'Brien and Thomas A. Shannon (Maryknoll, NY: Orbis Books, 1992), 60.
33. John Paul Szura, "Economic Rights and the Principle of Subsidiarity," in *Economic Justice: CTU's Pastoral Commentary on the Bishops' Letter on the Economy*, ed. John Pawlikowski and Donald Senior (Washington, DC: The Pastoral Press, 1988), 66.
34. Tanner makes a similar proposal in *Economy of Grace*, 128–29.
35. It is important to note, however, that Pius XI was scathingly critical of both capitalism and socialism as they were embodied in the early decades of the twentieth century. See *Quadragesimo Anno*, 51–59.
36. *Economic Justice for All*, 15.
37. "The basis for determining the value of human work is not primarily the kind of work being done but the fact that the one who is doing it is a person" (John Paul II, *Laborem Exercens*, in Miller, ed., *Encyclicals of John Paul II*, 175).
38. *Book of Confessions*, 10.3.

Index